"Bonnie and Mahesh a ... Spirit. They have huge, pu ... delight to be with because they love the presence of God. *Getting to Know the Holy Spirit* clearly flows out of their intimate friendship with God and out of living lives that are laid down for God's glory. I am thrilled to be able to recommend this book and pray that it leads many to become more intimately acquainted with the Holy Spirit."

—**Heidi Baker,** Ph.D., founding director, Iris Ministries

"Mahesh and Bonnie Chavda are two of my favorite people in the world partly because of how they joyfully model the theme of this book, *Getting to Know the Holy Spirit.* The Chavdas are known for prayer, passion, victorious living and absolute devotion to Christ. From my observation, all of these things flow from their relationship with the Holy Spirit. This book gives us a glimpse into one of the most sacred privileges in life: intimately knowing the third Person of the Trinity. It is practical, inspiring and revelatory. My heart burned as I read *Getting to Know the Holy Spirit.*"

—**Bill Johnson,** senior pastor of Bethel Church in Redding, California; author, *When Heaven Invades Earth* and *Face to Face with God*

"With biblical accuracy, contemporary testimonies and lives changed by the present-day ministry to the Holy Spirit, statesmen Mahesh and Bonnie Chavda bring us a classic in their book *Getting to Know the Holy Spirit.* With an equal mix of exposure to both the fruit and the gifts of the Holy Spirit, we are given a cutting-edge and yet balanced look at the third Person of the Godhead! I applaud Mahesh and Bonnie for living what they believe and helping the rest of us mature in the knowledge of God."

—**James W. Goll**, founder, Encounters Network and Prayer Storm International; author, *The Seer, The Lost Art of Intercession, The Coming Israel Awakening* and many others

GETTING TO KNOW THE

HOLY SPIRIT

MAHESH & BONNIE
CHAVDA

Published by Chosen Books
11400 Hampshire Avenue South
Bloomington, MN 55438
www.chosenbooks.com

Chosen Books is a division of
Baker Publishing Group, Grand Rapids, Michigan.

Printed in the United States of America

In keeping with biblical principles of creation stewardship, Baker Publishing Group advocates the responsible use of our natural resources. As a member of the Green Press Initiative, our company uses recycled paper when possible. The text paper of this book is comprised of 30% post-consumer waste.

green press INITIATIVE

Library of Congress Cataloging-in-Publication Data

Chavda, Mahesh, 1946–
    Getting to know the Holy Spirit / Mahesh & Bonnie Chavda.
        p.   cm.
    ISBN 978-0-8007-9471-2 (pbk. : alk. paper)   1. Holy Spirit.   I. Chavda, Bonnie.
II. Title.
    BT121.3.C545   2011
    231'.3—dc22

                                                                                2010041500

Dedicated to our Best Friend,
the Holy Spirit

Contents

Foreword

For nearly forty years now, Mahesh and Bonnie Chavda have been getting to know the Holy Spirit. I don't know anyone who is more qualified to teach on the Person of the Holy Spirit than Mahesh and Bonnie.

The first time I met Mahesh, my wife, Sharon, and I were invited to sing at a pastors' conference in Lagos, Nigeria. Mahesh was invited to be one of the speakers. I found out that he loved Jesus and loved country music—my kind of preacher! Mahesh was holding some healing meetings at night, so he asked if Sharon and I would come and sing some songs. We were good ol' Baptist kids, so we thought, "This will be great. We'll get out and meet some of the country folks."

So we sang a few songs, and then Mahesh got up and started to teach on the power of the Holy Spirit. Many in Africa knew of Mahesh because a few years before we were there, a little boy had been raised from the dead in one of his meetings. So there was great anticipation that the Holy Spirit would do something miraculous in these services. And He didn't disappoint!

While Mahesh was teaching, he stopped talking for a moment. Then he said, "I have a word from the Holy Spirit that there is a little girl here who was born blind, and tonight the Lord wants to heal you and give you sight." Well, I had never heard that kind of a word before, but sure enough, in a few minutes here came a little blind girl, with her mother and her aunt, onto the stage.

Mahesh said, "Ricky, come, let's see what the Holy Spirit is going to do for this little girl." So I walked over and stood close by. Mahesh didn't even touch her. He just prayed and asked the Lord to open her eyes and give her sight. He wanted the Holy Spirit to get all the credit for the miracle. I just stood there and watched as her eyes went from totally unfocused to focused. She looked at her hands. She looked at us strange men. Then she looked at her mother for the first time in her life.

But God never wastes a moment like that. I also received my sight that night as well. My eyes were opened to a power I had only read about. I've never been the same since. I'm still getting to know the Holy Spirit some twenty years later. It's a lifelong journey worth taking. This will be a great book for all of us who are getting to know the Holy Spirit!

Ricky Skaggs

Introduction

We are so happy to have an opportunity to talk with you about the best friend a human being can have. His name is the Holy Spirit of God. Every person has the opportunity to know Him in all His truth and love and beauty, but many people are still wondering and searching. Perhaps you have kept some distance from this mysterious Person of the Trinity. Perhaps you have met Him, and want to know Him more closely. Perhaps you want to discover the gifts He has given you and grow in their use.

Both of us had the privilege of discovering a personal relationship with God many years ago. We have each individually and together nurtured this relationship daily for nearly forty years. And we have learned that the way to have a true relationship with God is to get to know the Holy Spirit.

So it is with great joy that we anticipate that this book will help you deepen your relationship with God in a dynamic, relevant way.

We want you to know the possibility of personal fulfillment. We want you to be awakened to a fresh, confident and positive self-identity. We want you to consider—and maybe even believe—that you have a glorious personal destiny that is unique and beautiful and creative and special and important and valuable and eternal. We want you to have a whole heart, a healed heart, and a mind that is sound and at peace. We want you to move in power in your everyday life.

We want you to know that the Holy Spirit is a Person who brings you all these things and more. Your relationship with Him is the key to success, freedom and happiness.

Now, it is true that He is invisible and sometimes He is hidden, but He is always present and He is always working. He is *omni*—all—because He is God. He is omnipresent. He is omnipowerful. He is omni-knowledgeable. In the Person of the Holy Spirit, we see the beauty and splendor and power of God's divine nature. He is powerful but gentle, strong yet humble, truthful but encouraging. As you begin to see Him as He is, you will be able to look at your own history and find His footprints along your path.

What are you searching for? Are you searching for meaning in your life? Are you wondering why your life events have gone the way they have? Do you feel as though there must be more to life than what you have experienced so far?

No matter what your relationship or non-relationship with God is up to this point, *getting to know the Holy Spirit* is what you are looking for. He is who you need. He is the answer.

Amen,

Mahesh and Bonnie Chavda

Chapter 1

A Ghost, a Dove or a Person?

One evening when our oldest daughter Anna was in college, I, Mahesh, was suddenly overcome by a strong urge to pray. I did not know why, but I knew the Holy Spirit was alerting me and giving me this sense of urgency. I began to pray in the Spirit, and continued to pray for nearly three hours until I felt the inner prompting leave. It was late in the evening when I left my study, and I saw Anna's light was still on where she was preparing for her final exams. I stuck my head in the door to say good-night and heard myself saying, "Please drive your mother's Jeep instead of my car in the morning." She ordinarily drove my car to school every day. I had no particular reason to make the request, but when she nodded without looking up, I told her a second time just to make sure she had heard me. Then I went to bed.

The next morning, our phone rang just before eight o'clock. It was the police department. Our daughter Anna had just been involved in a terrible car crash.

When we arrived at the scene, the EMS and fire department were fervently working to extricate our daughter from the destroyed Jeep. She had hit a slick spot in the road and lost control of the vehicle. It was wrapped around a tree in a shallow ravine. Everyone involved was certain that our daughter was either dead or dying.

Bonnie rushed to the car as they finally got Anna out. The patrolman on the scene said, "It's a miracle your daughter is alive." He had never seen an accident like that where the driver had not been instantly killed. "Those airbags are what saved her life."(God)

We know that it was a lot more than airbags that protected our daughter that day. It was the presence of the Holy Spirit in our lives to guide and help us in crucial times that had watched over our daughter. I realized that my urgent need to pray the night before had been for my daughter's safety. I also realized that my instruction to drive her mother's Jeep came as a result of my time in prayer. My car was an older model and did not have airbags, but her mother's car did. I did not know any of the events that were about to happen, but my Friend the Holy Spirit did, and He was watching over my family and me.

Through experiences like that, both Bonnie and I have learned that we are utterly dependent upon the presence and guidance of the Holy Spirit. We have also learned just how much He cares for us, relates to us personally and is always there to give us the assistance we need. And He wants to relate to you, too.

About This Person

When we start thinking about the Holy Spirit, we have to realize He is a Person and not an "it." That means He has a specific personality. Let us describe Him to you.

The first thing to know about the Holy Spirit is probably this: He is happy. It is His nature to be joyful. It is also His nature to be humble, for He is very gentle. He is also powerful and strong, so when He comes alongside any one of us, He is able to fill up the places where we are empty; to heal the places where we are broken; to strengthen the places where we are weak. That is the very nature of the true God.

He has feelings and longings and desires. He is always at peace and He is everywhere.

King David wrote these words about God in one of his psalms:

> Where can I go from your Spirit?
> Or where can I flee from Your presence?
> If I ascend into heaven, You are there;
> If I make my bed in Sheol, behold, You are there.
> If I take the wings of the dawn,
> If I dwell in the remotest part of the sea,
> Even there Your hand will lead me,
> And Your right hand will lay hold of me.
>
> Psalm 139:7–10, NASB

Only God is omniscient (all-knowing), omnipotent (all-powerful), omnipresent (everywhere present). His Presence is His Spirit. This invisible and perceptible Presence permeates the entire universe. There is nowhere that He is not. He is present everywhere at the same time. No distance can separate you from Him; there is nowhere that you can go to be hidden from Him.

God knows everything. There is no place where things happen that He does not know about them. There is nothing you are facing—be it infirmity coming against your body or external circumstances or relational disaster or national crisis—that He has not already gained the victory over through His great power. Those who know Him have consolation in every situation because He does not change. *Amen., Glory to Jesus*

15

IN PERSON

Jesus told His disciples that there was going to be a divine exchange of Persons. He was going to the Father, and another Person was going to come be with us in His place.

He told them that there was an important reason for this: It was so that God would come to earth in the form of this Person called the Holy Spirit:

> "I am sending forth the promise of My Father upon you; but you are to stay in the city until you are clothed with power from on high. . . . The Helper, the Holy Spirit, whom the Father will send in My name, He will teach you all things, and bring to your remembrance all that I said to you."
>
> Luke 24:49, NASB; John 14:26, NASB

On the Day of Pentecost, the Holy Spirit was indeed poured out in all the earth. The Holy Spirit came to fulfill the ministry of Christ, teaching and being a companion to Jesus' followers.

This is an ongoing relationship so that we might hear the voice of the Lord and follow it. Jesus promised that everyone who believes in Him as Lord and Savior can be assured of knowing the Holy Spirit.

We can have a day-to-day personal relationship of happiness and fullness and beauty and the promise of eternal life in the Kingdom of glory—as we come to the Father, through the Son, by the power of the Holy Spirit.

Here are some other aspects of the Holy Spirit.

He Has Riches

The Holy Spirit is generous. He is a river without measure, continuously pouring out. Jesus said, "He will glorify Me, for He will take of what is Mine and declare it to you. All things that the Father has are Mine. Therefore I said that He will take of Mine and declare it to you" (John 16:14–15).

There are no "ifs, ands or buts" in that phrase. There are no bounds to what He can give. Jesus said, "All that I am, all that I have—here: It will come to you through the Spirit." What do you have faith for? He has the supply.

[handwritten margin note: GOD'S for all Salvation for All]

God has invested in us through the price of His Son, but there is even more. He has opened His bank and filled it with His Spirit, with Himself, and poured it out on His people in good measure. Now He is expecting satisfying returns on His investment. He is looking not just for leaves, but for fruit. Not just fruit, but character. Not just character, but wonderful signs of His power at work.

The Holy Spirit is the executor of the full inheritance of the riches of the Father and the Son, and without Him, as our friend and mentor Derek Prince used to say, "We can be heirs of the King and live like beggars."

We want to encourage you today to live like a king. If you are in total harmony with the King who resides within you, you have access to all of the riches of His Kingdom. And with that access you have authority to use them.

He Gives Comfort

After Jesus was resurrected from death to life, He told His disciples that He was going to leave them, and sorrow filled their hearts (see John 16:6). But He assured them that He was not going to leave them "comfortless." This word is connected to the idea of being an orphan.

Jesus put it this way. He said, "I tell you the truth. It is to your advantage that I go away; for if I do not go away, the Helper will not come to you; but if I depart, I will send Him to you" (John 16:7). In other words, it was in our best interests that He left, because then the Comforter would come.

Jesus made it plain that we are better off with Him in heaven reigning from His throne and the Holy Spirit with us here on earth, than with Him here and the Holy Spirit not given.

He Wrote the Bible

The Holy Spirit is the Author of the Bible. Your relationship with this Book reflects your relationship with the Living God. In other words, if you tend to question, doubt or pick apart every single line in the Bible, you may need to develop—or develop afresh—your relationship with its Author. The Bible came into being because holy men of old were borne along by the Spirit of God and wrote down what He said.

The Holy Spirit *plus* faith necessary for salvation *plus* the Bible are all intricately interconnected. And each is necessary in a dynamic, ongoing way in the believer's life.

It is wonderful to discover that, because He wrote it, when you read it He comes and looks over your shoulder and lets you know what He meant by it.

We could use the illustration of a grand piano—its keys being like the chapters and verses of the Bible. The Holy Spirit knows His instrument—every key, every note—and He knows exactly how to put them all together to make music that fills your heart. A song of love to woo you. A song of comfort when you are sorrowful. A song of courage when you are feeling timid. A song of joy when you are down and blue. And a song of the grandest beauty when this world seems dull and gray.

The Word of God is vitally important in relation to the Spirit. It is His transformation agent. He is watching out and watching over us to guide and help us, and to grow us up to be more like Jesus.

He Is the Indwelling Presence of God

The supreme promise of God is the indwelling of Christ Himself in our hearts by the power of the Holy Spirit. Put another way, God desires to live in us through the Spirit on the basis of our relationship with His Son.

We miss the real emphasis of the ministry of Jesus if we stop at His resurrection from the grave. Before Jesus returned to heaven He told His followers that that generation would see the coming of the Lord. What generation? It was the one that saw the redemptive purpose of God demonstrated when Jesus sent the Holy Spirit to believers.

The message was that we all can be made the residing place of God in the earth until Jesus comes again.

God predetermined that He would fashion us humans after the image of Christ. The supreme purpose for that physical body of yours is to serve as His dwelling place. As Paul wrote, "Do you not know that your body is the temple of the Holy Spirit who is in you?" (1 Corinthians 6:19).

He Is Holy

Jesus told His disciples that when the Holy Spirit arrived He would make people aware of any behavior that was not in keeping with goodness and righteousness. He said that the Holy Spirit would actually convict the world regarding the right way of thinking and living.

That is what we call morality and ethics, but it is instinctive in the nature of God. As the Holy Spirit comes to us, He makes us into new creatures with a set of values different from those of the natural mind.

We make a big mistake if we think we can do this ourselves, by human ability. We can understand or become partakers of holiness only insofar as we relate to God as He is.

God is unable to compromise *at all* in terms of anything untrue or evil or dark. His holiness will not mix or blend with anything less than the mark of absolute perfection. Those two things are like water and oil—by their very components they separate from each other.

We have been separated from God by our sin and we cannot restore that relationship by any means of our own. There are no good works we can do that will usher us into His presence.

This helps us to get a more proper grasp on why we need a Savior—and on the fact that Jesus came to save us from our sin. He gives us the clothing of Himself for every place we ever have or ever will miss the mark of being perfect people. When Jesus fills our hearts, God looks at us, sees His precious Son and opens His arms wide in welcome.

Because of Jesus, Hebrews 12:14 tells us to go for it: "Pursue peace with all people, and holiness, without which no one will see the Lord." We can run after God's holiness with all our strength.

He Is Your Friend

"I will talk to the Father," Jesus said to His followers, "and He'll provide you another Friend so that you will always have someone with you."

Different translations of the Bible use different words to describe this One who was to come. We like the word *The Message* offers here in John 14:15: *Friend.*

A little bit later, as Jesus continued to talk with His disciples about this provision from the Father, we get the impression that the coming of this Friend would be something like joyous fellowship, like the time around the harvest when everyone is filled with good things and feels peace and harmony.

"I didn't tell you this earlier," Jesus said, "because I was with you every day. But now I am on my way to the One who sent me. . . . I still have many things to tell you," Jesus continued, "but you can't handle them now. But when the Friend comes, the Spirit of the Truth, he will take you by the hand and guide you into all the truth there is. He won't draw attention to himself, but will make sense out of what is about to happen and, indeed, out of all that I have done and said" (John 16:4–5, 12–13, THE MESSAGE).

Have you ever needed a Friend to make a little sense out of what has happened or is happening—or perhaps is going to happen? Let us put your mind at ease. The help you receive will not necessarily be the world's common sense, but it will be the mind of God, the Spirit of Truth. This Friend will show you by revelation what is happening in the nations, what is happening in your life and heart, what is happening in your relationships, what is happening in your career.

We do not need to try to figure everything out. We need only resolve to enter into this Friend's company.

LOVE IN PERSON

The thirteenth chapter of First Corinthians gives a little biographical description of this Friend who loves you at all times. And look at the kind of Person He is.

Your Friend suffers long and is kind. Your Friend does not envy. Your Friend does not parade Himself around and is not "puffed up" with self-importance. Your Friend is not rude. Your Friend does not seek His own way. Your Friend does not provoke quarrels. Your Friend thinks no evil of you. Your Friend does not find it amusing when injustice or wickedness comes against you. Your Friend rejoices in the truth. Your Friend—and this is a lovely verse—bears all things.

This is a description of the true God and the Spirit of Truth whom He has sent. He has faith in you. He has faith in His promise in you. He has confidence in the power of the blood covenant that Jesus has cut with you through His death on the cross. Your Friend hopes all things. Your Friend endures all things. Your Friend never fails.

He never fails.

That is our Friend, the Holy Spirit. And that will be the fruit of His work and His presence in your life. He believes in you. He hopes that all the promises of God will be fulfilled in you. He bears up under every circumstance and hangs with you "in spite of." He endures day to day with you, even in your worst times.

He never fails.

It is our purpose in this book to help you "see" the Holy Spirit as this Person. As we journey along, you will discover how fruit is formed in a life that He indwells and better understand the gifts He has for you. You will find that your comprehension of how this Friend relates to you and how you relate to Him grows. You will learn to walk with fresh vigor into a life of holiness—not because you have to, but because you want to.

As you experience the power of Christ living in you through the Holy Spirit, you will have the opportunity to realize that wholeness and happiness really are available for you.

We pray that your heart and imagination and desires will be touched in a way that moves you to want God in a new and living companionship. We pray that you really get to know the Holy Spirit.

Prayer

Father God, I thank You that through the finished work of Your Son, my Savior, Jesus Christ, I can be filled with Your Holy Spirit. Wonderful Holy Spirit, I welcome You into my life. I desire to know You with all my heart. I receive You as my Best Friend, my Guide, my Comforter. I open my heart to Your presence. Teach me Your ways, blessed Holy Spirit, so that I may be an emissary of Your love and mercy.

Chapter 2

Invisible Friend

Everyone has a hero. Yours might be a sports figure, an entertainer or a political figure past or present. It may even be a character from literature. When you think of your hero, you imagine what he or she looks like, how they act and what they would say to you if you knew them personally. Now imagine one day there's a knock at your door and you open it to see your hero standing there. Your hero introduces himself or herself and says, "I want to get to know you personally. Let's strike up a lifelong friendship."

The Holy Spirit is a person who knows you well. He has been seeking you, whether you have known it or not. Often we do not realize this until He makes Himself known in some dramatic way.

Bible Pictures

Friendship with someone who is invisible can be a challenge. Since the Holy Spirit cannot be seen with our eyes, the Bible gives us a number of images to help us get to know Him. These images aid our understanding. When the Bible calls Him the "Holy Ghost," it is referring to Him as a Person who is a spirit with a personality and who is God Himself. Though He is all-powerful, He is not scary or evasive. He is a loving, faithful companion seeking you out because He wants to be your friend.

The Dove

One of the first images we think of when we contemplate the Holy Spirit is the dove. A dove is gentle, primarily. The first recorded sermon that Jesus preached—after the Holy Spirit had descended on Him in the form of a dove at His baptism in the Jordan River—gives us an idea of this gentleness.

In the synagogue the scroll of the prophet Isaiah was handed to Jesus, and He opened it to these words and read:

> The Spirit of the Lord GOD is upon Me,
> Because the LORD has anointed Me
> To preach good tidings to the poor;
> He has sent Me to heal the brokenhearted,
> To proclaim liberty to the captives,
> And the opening of the prison to those who are bound;
> To proclaim the acceptable year of the LORD.
>
> Isaiah 61:1–2

God is thoughtful of the poor and the brokenhearted and the prisoner. He is comfortable around people who have humble, compassionate hearts, who are not harsh or rude.

That may be one of the biggest mysteries about our God, and it is modeled in the image of a dove: God does not rule through domination. He could, and He would be perfectly righteous in so doing. But because He is love, He does not rule by force.

He does not even impose His Presence where He is not wanted. He always waits to be received, and when He stops being received, He waits patiently outside the door until He is welcomed back in.

This is one of the most astounding things about His nature, and the Holy Spirit exemplifies it.

The Teacher

Luke tells us that when he wrote the gospel that bears his name, he endeavored to record "all that Jesus began both to do and teach" (Acts 1:1). Jesus taught by doing and by telling stories, but before He taught He learned. He underwent training—not only from His parents, for He was subject to them while growing up, but also from the Holy Spirit.

Jesus performed His miracles—He worked out His ministry, so to speak—under the anointing of the Holy Spirit. He did the things the Holy Spirit impressed on Him, letting the Holy Spirit lead Him, empower Him, enable Him, guide Him, and all was done in communion with the Father. Luke 10:21 gives us a picture of this tri-unity at work: While rejoicing in the Holy Spirit, Jesus raised His voice in praise of the Father.

There is a beautiful illustration of our walk with the Holy Spirit in the story of the Austrian Von Trapp family, notably adapted in the film *The Sound of Music.*

A widowed naval officer and father of seven children, Captain Von Trapp runs his home much like a ship with a crew—strict rules, schedules, even uniforms.

The children are starving for love and joy but none of them realizes it until Maria, who desires to be a nun, accepts the position of governess and begins teaching the children. Maria introduces them to singing and joyful romps and picnics around the countryside, inspiring them to find joy in the smallest things.

The children fall in love with life—and with Maria. Captain Von Trapp grows closer to his children than ever before when his eyes are opened to the beauty and freedom Maria brings them—particularly as dark clouds of Hitler's regime begin to swirl around them. Ultimately the captain and Maria marry and, with the children, face the future with courage.

This story is a wonderful picture of the Holy Spirit coming into regimented, drab or powerless lives. The Holy Spirit comes to teach us about God, about ourselves, about the world. We all need a teacher, and what better teacher to have than the One who knows everything?

Flames of Fire

The Bible tells us that when the Holy Spirit came at Pentecost, He came as the image of fire. Through the emblem of fire we can perceive that His presence can get stronger and brighter, ever more enflamed. This shows how He purges us from sin and evil, and builds us up in the image of Jesus Christ.

Flames can also be quenched. The more we do things that are displeasing to Him, the more our Friend lifts away from us and the less we will shine.

We are keepers of the flame in our personal lives—and in our corporate life together with other believers. Paul wrote to the Thessalonian church telling them not to "quench the Spirit," not to put out its flame (see 1 Thessalonians 5:19).

As we obtain salvation through Jesus Christ, we learn to do the things that please Him. Here are a few taken from the fifth chapter of Ephesians. We should:

- comfort one another
- build each other up
- honor the ones who labor in our midst for the Gospel
- honor our spiritual leaders; esteem them highly in love
- be at peace

- warn those who are unruly
- comfort the feeble-minded
- support the weak
- be patient toward everyone
- never give back evil for evil
- always follow the good path

The Holy Spirit is seeking to brighten the lives of those who are quick to rejoice, who pray without ceasing, who always find a reason to give thanks. We soon find that giving honor to God by the way we live pleases Him. This is being a steward of the flame.

Holy Oil

In Old Testament days before the Temple was built in Jerusalem, the place that God had appointed to meet face-to-face with humankind was the Tabernacle.

With all of the other specific instructions about the construction of this large tent and its contents, God told Moses to make a specific kind of oil for the various ceremonies and services of worship and gave him the recipe (it is found in Exodus 30:22–33).

It was to be made of liquid myrrh, fragrant cinnamon, sweet-smelling cane, cassia and olive oil. God was very particular about how to put these elements together to make the oil—"an ointment compounded according to the art of the perfumer" (Exodus 30:25)—and the people were forbidden to make this oil for any other use, for anything it touched became holy.

This holy anointing oil consecrated everything that went into the Tabernacle, including the priests. So even though God is kind and generous to all, without the consecration of the anointing oil no one was allowed into His presence.

The Holy Spirit is available to every believer in Jesus, and this indicates that we have full access to enter God's presence and are anointed as a royal priesthood to demonstrate His goodness to the earth (see 1 Peter 2:9).

The components of the oil were symbolic of the events that would occur in the life of Jesus. Myrrh is *mara* in Hebrew, which means "bitter," but the aroma is actually wonderful. When the wise men came and worshiped baby Jesus, they prepared Him prophetically for His death and burial through the gift of myrrh.

Another element in the oil, cassia, is a very sweet and very rare herb. It releases its fragrance as it is crushed or bruised. The prophet Isaiah foretold how the Savior, the Messiah, would be "crushed" to pay the price for our sinfulness (see Isaiah 53:5, NASB).

The Counselor

The Old Testament gives types of the Holy Spirit as our personal guide and counselor. Naomi in the book of Ruth is a type of the Holy Spirit personally leading us to Jesus and our inheritance.

Ruth was a childless widow in a famished land the day she left her heritage, her home and her country to follow her mother-in-law, Naomi, back to her homeland. As she attended to Naomi and followed her direction, she caught the eye and heart of Boaz, the most prosperous man in town. He was her kinsman redeemer. Ruth's attention to Naomi's instruction gave her adoption into the family of God, a future, a hope and an inheritance. Ruth became a mother in the lineage of our Kinsman Redeemer, Jesus.

Another type of the Holy Spirit is the eunuch in the book of Esther. The eunuch was in charge of the fairest women of the Persian empire, all gathered for the beauty contest whose winner would become queen. He oversaw the yearlong process of beautifying and training the women to please the king.

Like the eunuch, the Holy Spirit never claims or plans to make

His own lineage, but is the faithful steward of God's Kingdom. He gives counsel, gifts, washings, beautification, outfitting us to sit as queen beside the King of Glory for eternity.

The Unnamed Servant

When Abraham determined the time was right to find a bride for his only son, Isaac, he gave the task to an unnamed servant, who "ruled over all that he had" (Genesis 24:2). He was the steward of all of Abraham's wealth, and yet he is never named in this story. It is a picture of the Holy Spirit. He never draws attention to Himself. He is always drawing attention to the Father and pointing to the Bridegroom, Jesus.

Abraham sent his servant with a caravan of ten camels loaded with gifts of gold and riches to bless the family of the bride the servant would choose. The Holy Spirit is God's representative on the earth. He is the resident Lord of God's family on earth, in charge of His entire household. He is seeking the eternal Bride for Jesus, God's Son. We who believe in Him are that Bride. He is adorning us with gifts and blessings as a guarantee of the riches to come when we see our Bridegroom face-to-face.

UP CLOSE AND PERSONAL

These are a few of the images that help us picture the Holy Spirit, and even though we do not see Him the way we see a sunset or an orchard, we understand that He sometimes lets us sense His presence and His person in physical ways that encourage or bless us.

Sometimes in worship services people tell of catching the scent of some sweet fragrance. The Holy Spirit's presence seems tangible on such occasions. If He chooses He can easily give us more discerning senses—hearing, seeing and even smelling—in order to help us perceive a dimension beyond the natural one we live in. We can sense His closeness as He anoints us for worship.

This was the case with a young woman named Jennifer who told us her story.

> I was looking everywhere for God, because my sister was dying of cancer, and I had no answers. I had grown up Catholic but had left the church for about fifteen years. I was going to a New Age church, even though I knew God probably wasn't in a New Age church.
>
> I really didn't know I was looking for the God of the Bible, but I asked a friend of mine who read the Bible every day how she knew that it talked about the one and only true God. She told me, "If you'll just ask God, He'll reveal Himself to you." I didn't know what she meant, so I kept asking her about it. I took this woman to lunch for weeks drilling her with questions.
>
> Then one day when I was driving home by myself I just cried out, "God, please help me!" At that moment the Holy Spirit came into my car and filled me to the top of my head. And then a strong pair of arms encircled me and hugged me.
>
> God knew I needed a tangible experience at that point in my life. I know now without a doubt that I had met the one and only true God.

God is not separate from the physical world in which we live. When Jesus returned to heaven and the Holy Spirit came, for instance, it was actually a physical exchange. It was spiritual and supernatural, but it was also physical in that another Person who is the fire and fragrance of God Almighty literally came to indwell us.

Let's look at an incident from the life of Moses told in Exodus 33–34. During the wilderness wanderings of the children of Israel, before they entered the Promised Land, God would meet with Moses and give him various instructions for the people to follow.

On one occasion Moses asked God to show him His glory. God agreed and told Moses to meet Him at the top of Mount Sinai and then go to a certain rock, adding that when His glory was passing by, God would put Moses in the cleft of the rock under the safe cover of His hand.

It happened as God had said. Moses saw the spectacle of God's glory, then bowed low toward the earth, worshiping. The sight he saw, which we imagine as light, was not just a demonstration of nature; it was actually nature reflecting the presence of a Person, a Person who had called Moses into His Presence.

We read as the story goes on that, oddly enough, being in that Presence sustained Moses physically for some time. He did not need to eat or drink for forty days because he was in the embrace of the source of life.

When he came down from the mountain after that experience, Moses himself was glowing like a lightning bug from having been in the Presence. What a beautiful revelation of the true nature of God! The Holy Spirit comes to bless others by revealing the Presence of the Lord of glory, the Creator of the universe.

Paul mentioned this experience of Moses, saying that the Israelites could not even look steadily at Moses' face when he returned back down the mountain because of the "glory of his countenance" (2 Corinthians 3:7). Inner beauty comes out from us as we fellowship with the Holy Spirit and get to know Him. He saturates us and we cannot help but show it.

Building Intimacy

If, then, we understand that the Holy Spirit is a Person, if we see Him in Bible pictures, if we experience Him in physical senses and if we let Him light our way to the Father, what is our response?

Or put another way, once we understand that friendship is possible with the invisible God, what do we do?

Paul wrote to the believers in Rome stating that "the love of God has been poured out in our hearts by the Holy Spirit" (Romans 5:5). He is the agent by which God has chosen to pour out His love. The natural response to love is to love back the one who loves you.

This is where intimacy comes in. Intimacy is love responding to love. People do this all the time on a human level, and it is no different with God Almighty. God is holy, but He is also love. We love because He is love. He is love, and He is an agent of love.

Think of a committed married couple. The husband learns what makes his wife happy or sad, just as the wife learns about her husband. In the same manner, we are dwelling on a long-term basis with the most wonderful Person we will ever have in our lives—One who is totally committed to us, who wants to be our Best Friend, the most loyal, faithful Friend who will never leave unless we keep insisting that we do not want Him.

As we develop a friendship with the Holy Spirit, He makes us more like the Lord Jesus Christ. He forms us into His image. That is what the Bible means when it talks about looking into the glory, "beholding as in a mirror the glory of the Lord" (2 Corinthians 3:18). We are being transformed from glory to glory.

What is that transformation leading to? What is the end product? It is to be made in the image of Jesus Christ, to more fully represent the Lord: His character, His love, His gentleness, His humility, His heart of a servant. Those and many other things.

We cannot continue to walk with this Friend without being formed and transformed because that is His purpose. His goal is to form a perfect people for Jesus, who will return like a Bridegroom coming for His Bride.

The character of Christ is the example for us as we are being transformed by this relationship of love.

DON'T GRIEVE YOUR BEST FRIEND

If we choose not to respond to the love of God poured out through the Holy Spirit, our actions will eventually lead to His distress. Because the Holy Spirit is a Person who relates to us with deep love, we can do and say things or act in ways that suppress harmony and happiness with Him—just as would happen in any relationship.

A verse in Isaiah talks about certain people who did this: "They rebelled and vexed his Holy Spirit. Therefore, he was turned to be their enemy and he fought against them" (Isaiah 63:10). Wow! They vexed Him. Their ongoing carnal responses in their lives offended the Holy Spirit, and God's friendship was lifted from them.

"Do not grieve the Holy Spirit of God" (Ephesians 4:30). The Holy Spirit is holy, and therefore it is possible for Him to be grieved by sin. He is not touchy; He is holy.

Hebrews 10:29 says that people can *insult* the Spirit of grace and connects it with trampling the blood of Christ underfoot. The reference is directly related to vexing the Holy Spirit as described in the above verse from Isaiah.

People often wonder as they begin their walk with God if they have somehow blasphemed Him. They worry about having committed the "unpardonable sin" and grieving Him beyond repair.

Matthew 12:31–37 shows us clearly that this happens when we deliberately and knowingly attribute satanic action to the Holy Spirit of God. Giving the devil credit for God's work leads to blasphemy against the Holy Spirit.

In many decades of dealing with human problems we have never

personally encountered anyone who has committed the unpardonable sin, though we have helped to comfort and instruct a number
of persons who thought they had unwittingly done so.

When the blood of Jesus was shed, it made provision for us to
be born again and be rid of that innate, guilty conscience that we
inherited as descendants of Adam. It is safe to say that, other than
stumbling and falling into some kind of royal mess-up, guilt is the
biggest barrier to walking in absolute liberty in the Holy Spirit. It
is the biggest block to moving in His power.

Guilt comes from a sense of having broken God's law, but
remember: Condemnation is pseudo-guilt. The Holy Spirit con-
victs of sin. He never condemns. It is the devil who accuses, the
flesh that condemns.

When God is speaking to us about adjustments in our lives,
it comes in a manner of conviction. It is clean. It is peaceful. It is
hope-filled. It carries the full assurance of faith. It speaks of a clear
way for deliverance and release and victory: through the blood of
Calvary.

The more we practice being loving persons the less we miss the
mark. That makes Him happy and will make us happy, too, because
we were made to be in happy relationship with God.

Our Job: Cultivate the Relationship

What pleases our Friend the Holy Spirit? That we grow to be
more like Jesus. In one of His times of teaching Jesus said that a bad
tree cannot bear good fruit. If it is no longer fit for use, it will be cut
down and thrown into the fire (see Matthew 7:19).

Our job is to keep cultivating this friendship with the Holy
Spirit. If we get disappointed or flounder in our walk and wonder

why we are not bearing fruit, it is usually because we have neglected to work on our love relationship with the Lord.

If we may say it this way, it is as though the Holy Spirit is allergic to certain things—like anger, bitterness, criticism, gossip. They will cause Him to wait outside for us until we make the decision to walk in a Christ-like manner.

If we want to be friends with Him, we must do what is pleasing, speak that which is pleasing, behave ourselves and conduct ourselves in such a manner that He is happy to fellowship with us.

And as we do, we will find that every "coincidence," every moment of grace or sensation of His presence, every moment of joy is a moment when the omni-God in the Person of the Holy Spirit is present and revealing Himself.

Ultimately, it is not true that all roads lead to God. But we can say that the Holy Spirit is present to walk with us down all the roads of our lives with the intention of bringing us to the ultimate destination: fullness of relationship with God.

We will never truly be fulfilled in this life because we were made for immortality. Nothing here will fully satisfy because we are heading on to glory. And it is our Friend who helps us along.

Prayer

Lord, I pray that You will make my heart tender to every nudge from the Holy Spirit. Tune my ears to hear the gentlest whisper from my Best Friend. Help me love that which He loves, and shun that which grieves Him. Open the eyes of my heart to recognize Him in my daily walk. May I conduct my life, my thoughts and my speech in such a manner that my Friend is pleased to abide with me.

Chapter 3

NEW BEGINNING

There is a story told of a man named Vince Lombardi, an almost indomitable American football coach. He was hired by a downtrodden Green Bay Packers organization to try to turn the team around; the Packers had had losing seasons for years. The previous year they had won only one game.

Coach Lombardi called his new team together and rose to speak. After a moment's pause, he held a football way up high and said, "Gentlemen, this is a football."

Getting back to basics took that team from the worst in the league to two-time National Football League champions.

If you never thought of the Holy Spirit as one with whom you can have a primary personal relationship, this is a wonderful new beginning for you! In this chapter we are going to hold the Bible way up high and look at the basics to discover what it says about "baptism with the Holy Spirit." We are going to explore what it means, why we need it and how to get it.

A STUNNING EXPERIENCE: PENTECOST

One Sunday in the early spring, close to two thousand years ago, the disciples of Jesus were gathered in a room on one of the upper floors of a building in Jerusalem. Ten days earlier, Jesus had ascended into heaven—He had literally risen up before their eyes, entering the clouds above their heads. Now they were waiting in Jerusalem as He had instructed them.

Suddenly, a sound came from heaven . . .

> as of a rushing mighty wind, and it filled the whole house where they were sitting. Then there appeared to them divided tongues, as of fire, and one sat upon each of them. And they were all filled with the Holy Spirit and began to speak with other tongues, as the Spirit gave them utterance.
>
> Acts 2:2–4

The first thing the first ones got when they received this wonderful river was joy. They became "drunk" with the Spirit (see Acts 2:15). Hand in hand with that joy came courage from heaven (see Acts 4:31). The whole community that had been cowering for fear of persecution joyously went out in the streets to tell of the wonderful works of Jesus—in the same city where they had seen Him crucified.

Fearlessness drove out fear when the Holy Spirit came in power. A new certainty of the future, both personal and community-wide, gave them a new perspective. What life had been was nothing when compared to the power from heaven they now possessed.

People from all over the world were in Jerusalem at this time for the festival. They were drawn to the commotion and were astonished to hear these Galileans speaking in all of their different languages. They could not begin to imagine what was going on, so they came to a conclusion: These people must be drunk!

But Peter stood before them and preached what was perhaps his greatest sermon. With boldness he declared:

"Fellow Israelites, listen carefully to these words: Jesus the Nazarene, a man thoroughly accredited by God to you—the miracles and wonders and signs that God did through him are common knowledge—this Jesus, following the deliberate and well-thought-out plan of God, was betrayed by men who took the law into their own hands, and was handed over to you. And you pinned him to a cross and killed him. But God untied the death ropes and raised him up. Death was no match for him."

Acts 2:22–24, THE MESSAGE

Now, when the crowd heard this, they were cut to the heart. This tells us, by the way, that the message of the Bible should affect our hearts. It is not just head knowledge. It is like falling in love. You kind of lose your senses because your heart belongs to someone else now.

Just so, when you see Jesus, you fall in love. You are cut to the heart. It is the greatest love we will ever know. And when your heart belongs to Jesus, there is no price too high to pay to serve Him.

The crowd, their hearts stirred, asked this question: "What shall we do?" They now understood that God the Father loved them so much He had sent His only Son on their behalf. They saw that they could have light and eternal life. They were willing to do anything.

Peter knew the answer. Through him the apostolic word came:

"Change your life. Turn to God and be baptized, each of you, in the name of Jesus Christ, so your sins are forgiven. Receive the gift of the Holy Spirit. The promise is targeted to you and your children, but also to all who are far away—whomever, in fact, our Master God invites."

Acts 2:38–39, THE MESSAGE

He was saying to the crowd, "If you have any sense of who Jesus is, and you want to turn your life over to Him and live with Him for all of eternity, then here are three things that you need to do: Repent, be baptized and receive the Holy Spirit."

The crowd of people from every nation responded. About three thousand people, who now believed in Jesus, were baptized that day and received the Holy Spirit as a gift. As Jesus had prophesied, the Gospel was now beginning to reach out from His small band of disciples into all the world.

Let's look at these three points that Peter delineated. They are offered to us, just as to that crowd in Jerusalem.

First, Make a Change

Repentance means basically a change of direction. Change your mind. Change your way of thinking. Change your approach to life, and adopt God's perspective and mode of operation. You were going in one direction, but now you are going in the opposite direction. It does not matter if you are from Russia or Chile or Indonesia or Canada or the United States or Zimbabwe or China. All have sinned and come short of the glory of God (see Romans 3:23). All are under the kingdom of darkness until the light of the Gospel comes.

It also does not matter if your parents were Buddhist, Christian, Jewish, Islamic, Hindu or atheists. There is no special entry into God's Kingdom based on heritage. Each and every one of us—in every nation, every tribe, every language—has sinned.

So what direction do we want to face? At one time we had no choice. We all had our backs to God. We were facing the kingdom of darkness. We belonged under the authority of Satan.

But God showed mercy to us. He gave us His Son, who lived

a sinless life and died sacrificially that we might be reconciled to the Father.

When you repent you turn around. You turn your back on Satan and his kingdom of darkness, and you face the Kingdom of God and His light.

You say, "Yes, Lord, You are my Lord. You are my God. Jesus, You are the King of Glory. Jesus, I repent of my sins. I receive You. Cleanse me in Your blood."

As we will learn in chapter 6 on fruit of the Spirit, it soon becomes clear that repentance is not only the way we are facing; repentance also involves the way we are walking. In other words, repentance is not just a thing of emotional good intentions. Emotions are fine. But if someone just gets emotional and there is no change in his or her life, then it shows that the person has not truly repented.

If, for instance, a man who is an alcoholic and beats his wife says he has repented of his evil, but then he goes home and heads for the liquor cabinet and beats his wife again, has repentance come? No. He has had no change of heart. If a woman says she has repented of bad behavior, but then continues to gossip and connive and manipulate to get her way, has repentance come? No. She has had no change of heart.

People will always make mistakes, of course, but in general the fruit that repentance bears is a changed life—a change of lifestyle, a change in desire, a change in heart.

When I, Mahesh, made this confession that I wanted to repent for all the ways I had sinned and wanted to trust God with my life, I no longer wanted to hang around with the people I was mostly friends with. They were good people, but they were so intellectual they had no use for the concept of a righteous and holy God who would judge sin.

They thought Christians were fanatics. So I said, "I'm going to hang out with the fanatics." I loved talking about Jesus with like-minded people. My "taste" changed. I became identified with Jesus.

Further, Jesus told His followers that they must repent and believe the Gospel. Without repentance, then, we cannot believe what the Bible says. Those who say they do not believe the Bible have never repented.

We must repent if we want fellowship with God. Without it we will perish. We will face an eternal existence away from His presence. This is not a question of bigotry or intolerance; it is a question of obedience.

But if we are willing to submit to the principles of the Bible, we also can confidently claim its promises. Peter, in his sermon that Pentecost Sunday, said that the promise of God is for all of us and our children. When people in the New Testament believed that Jesus was who He said He was and chose to repent from unbelief, the knowledge of Him seemed to explode in that person's whole house! God is a God of household salvation.

Acts 17:30 says that God "now commands all men everywhere to repent." We believe what the Word of God says about us. We have sinned. We are all sinners. We need a Savior. We need Christ.

God stands ready and waiting for us to make this decision. He says to you, "Hey, I want to bless you. Come home. Come home."

Second, Take a Bath

A wise man—a priest, in fact—named Nicodemus came to Jesus. The conversation went something like this:

"Jesus, this changed lifestyle you're talking about is impossible. A person would have to start all over, go back to the point of his beginning—back to his mother's womb—and be born all over again."

Jesus answered, "That's exactly right! But this time, this rebirth happens by a miracle. It is the work of the Holy Spirit. Every person who has been born of a woman must also be born of the Spirit."

I, Mahesh, was a Hindu. In my family I could trace back for eight hundred years the names of family members who were Hindu. When I repented and gave my life to Jesus, I made this confession in front of everybody. On the east coast of Africa in the city of Mombasa, I walked into the Indian Ocean and got baptized. A missionary pastor baptized me publicly before hundreds of people. I could have been killed, but I loved Jesus so much.

The distinguishing sign of the decision to repent, along with a changed lifestyle, is water baptism. This is the outward act demonstrating that there has been an inward change. Through this expression of faith you are identifying with the death, burial and resurrection of the Lord Jesus Christ. You are saying publicly that you do not belong to darkness, you belong to light.

Water baptism is a visible demonstration. It is like a bride walking down the aisle. Our older daughter got married recently and took the last name of her husband. Just so, in the exercise of water baptism you officially take the name of your divine Bridegroom, Jesus.

In addition He gives you the legal right to write checks on His account. Everything that belongs to Jesus belongs to you—including His authority. Jesus said, "All authority has been given to Me in heaven and on earth. Go, therefore, in the power of that authority" (see Matthew 28:18).

Sometimes our team will go to minister in a city and someone will say, "Did you sense the darkness there in that wicked city?" And we will say, "Those things bow to us; we don't bow to them."

Wherever you are there may be darkness, there may be perversion, there may be any number of reasons to believe in the devil. But those things bow to you as you walk in the marvelous light and power of the Holy Spirit. You change the equation. If there is a sense of depression, depression does not stay there when you are there. If oppression seems to rule, it does not stay around you. Those things bow to the authority of Jesus' name. That name belongs to you.

The First Baptism in the Bible

Remember our history, friends, and be warned. All our ancestors were led by the providential cloud and taken miraculously through the Sea. They went through the waters, in a baptism like ours, as Moses led them from enslaving death to salvation life.

1 Corinthians 10:1–2, The Message

When Moses led the Israelites out of slavery in Egypt through the desert toward the Promised Land, a great pillar that looked like a cloud shielded them from the sun. By night that pillar became fire, protecting and warming them. It led them in their journey, going on ahead of them when they were supposed to move to a new location.

You will recall in this familiar story that, at an earlier point, soon after the Israelites had left Egypt, Pharaoh regretted that he had let them go free. He called out his powerful army and went off in hot pursuit.

The Israelites came up against the shores of the Red Sea. Looking back, they saw the clouds of dust from Pharaoh's approaching army. They were trapped. Death seemed imminent.

Then Moses stretched forth his staff, and the sea parted before them. All of the Israelites, more than a million people, walked safely through the waters, which were piled high on either side of them.

When the Egyptians chased them into the dry riverbed, the waters came crashing down and the army was drowned.

This true story demonstrates that something remarkable happens in water baptism. When you leave the old life, passing through the Red Sea waters of baptism, the waters close behind you and drown all those enemies of the past.

Going into the baptismal water is like being buried. And in that burial, all of the past identity, the past life, the past shadows, everything about your past dies. The heart that previously has been asleep or dull or hard or cold or not fully awakened to God is cut away by the hand of the Holy Spirit.

Then, you come up out of the water a glorious new creation. Now the Holy Spirit can write His Word on your new heart day by day.

By the way, it is scriptural to get baptized a second time. No one has to, but if the Holy Spirit tells you to, you can. Sometimes people are baptized as infants or children and do not really understand how much it means. When they get older, some may want to go through the experience again with the full impact of its meaning.

In Scripture, as we just saw, the children of Israel were baptized in the Red Sea experience. But then forty years later they were baptized once again when the Jordan River parted before them and they walked through carrying the Ark of the Covenant. They were coming into the Promised Land provision.

If people feel that the Promised Land has not been there for them or there seem to be some Egyptians still trailing on their tail, and if the Holy Spirit tells them to be water baptized again, they are free to do so.

Baptism in the Congo River

I, Mahesh, held a baptismal service in Kinshasa in the Congo many years ago. Prior to that baptismal service, a great throng of people had listened to the Word of God being preached, and many thousands had come forward to profess their new faith in Jesus Christ. We saw some amazing things happen.

About three thousand of them wanted to be baptized, but I did not know how to baptize so many. I come from a tradition in which we use baptismal "tanks," such as you might see up in the front of some churches.

So I said to the Lord, "Well, gosh, how are we going to baptize all these people? What are we going to do?"

And I sensed that the Lord said, *I have provided a tank for you.*

I said, "Well, if You provided a tank, You have not told me."

Quite clearly I heard Him say, *It's called the River Congo.*

The Congo River was a border region between the Republic of Congo—it was called Zaire at the time—and Brazzaville.

I had to get permission from the government to hold a water baptismal service. It was difficult to get. One of the men among the families that had come to Christ under my ministry was a general of the Army of the Congo. He and his family had been wonderfully touched by the Lord. So I went to his house and said, "I want to get permission to hold a big baptismal service in the Congo River."

He said, "All right, I'll get it for you, but you have to take more soldiers with you."

I said, "No soldiers, we don't need soldiers—this is a religious service."

He said, "Soldiers. You take soldiers."

I said, "No soldiers."

He said, "No soldiers, no service."

I said, "Yes, sir. Soldiers."

So we got permission for the service, and thousands gathered at the river. They were all singing—it was wonderful. About 150 area pastors were helping us with the baptisms. I had seen some of the tributaries there, but they were nothing like the Congo River.

I remember that I was wearing a new pair of Nike jogging shoes. I went into the river and had forgotten that centuries of sediment had settled along its bed. My feet started sinking; actually, the river bottom was sucking my feet in. I had to drag myself further out into the river. Somewhere in the river one of my shoes was sucked up, and moments later the other one was sucked up. But I kept going until I was waist-deep in the river.

After a few moments I slowly sank into gunk up almost to my knees. I could not move. Then I heard guns being fired and saw that the soldiers were shooting their machine guns all around me. I said, "Oh, Jesus, what are those crazy soldiers doing?"

As I swung my head around to see what they were shooting at, I noticed some logs floating around me. But then I saw one of the logs open its mouth. "These are not logs," I said somewhat in shock. "Those are crocodiles!"

The Lord had neglected to tell me that crocodiles were living in that river. It was one of the times that I knew the implications of serving Him. Sometimes He tells you to do something, and He hands you a piece of paper and says, "Sign here at the bottom." And you say, "But the page is empty." And He says, "Yes, I'll fill it in later."

When I signed up for the Lord, one of the things He filled in later was "Water baptism in crocodile-infested water."

So the soldiers kept firing their guns, and the brave and happy people, all singing, came out to us to be baptized. More than three thousand people were baptized that day. We still have their names in our office. We have pictures and videos of that awesome and, as far as I know, historic event in the Congo River. I will never forget that day.

There was one woman who made a particularly startling

impression. Many of those people had long ancestries of witchcraft. They had been driven for generations by demons of darkness and oppression. This young woman, who lived there in the bush, had been dominated by that evil and was no longer in her right mind. She had lived most of her life like a wild animal: She would run around and bite people. She ate whatever food people threw at her.

Wearing nothing but a big T shirt with holes, she saw us baptizing people and thought in her crazy mind that we were swimming. So she ran down the hill and started screaming, "I want to swim! I want to swim!"

She headed toward some of the pastors who were farther down from me—we were all stretched in a line—and kept screaming, "I want to swim! I want to swim!"

The pastors there said, "Come on in," and the ushers, partly lifting, partly dragging, helped her reach them. It is good they did not ask my permission because I probably would have said no! But they just took her by the arms and said, "We baptize you in the name of the Lord Jesus Christ." Then, boom, they put her down in the water.

When she came up out of the water, she was a different person. She was in her right mind and completely delivered from the darkness that had plagued her. Her deliverance was a stunning display of the power of God in the celebration of water baptism.

Two years later on another trip to the Congo I had just stepped off the plane when one of the stewardesses from the flight approached me and said, "Do you recognize me?"

I said, "No, who are you?"

She said, "I'm the woman who got delivered in the Congo River."

It was so wonderful to see what the Holy Spirit had done in her life. He works that way in every life—each new heart is a dramatic declaration of His power to heal and deliver.

Water baptism has been purchased for us through the most expensive price ever paid: the blood of Jesus. There is no element in the universe more expensive. You can pile all the gold, diamonds, emeralds, pearls, all the financial empires of the countries of the world and put them on one side, and put one drop of the blood of Jesus on the other side, and say, "Which is more powerful?" And there is no comparison. One drop of the blood of Jesus saves us and destroys every stronghold that would oppress us.

The price has been paid; therefore, you can receive the blessings of your inheritance in Jesus. The more you have a revelation of the blood of Jesus shed at Calvary, the more you will be able to walk in your inheritance.

If you have never been baptized, now is the time. Get connected to a local church that believes in Jesus and the full Gospel presented in the Bible, a church where you can be baptized. Bury your old life and come up as a new creation.

THIRD, COME, HOLY SPIRIT!

When you repent of your sins and ask Jesus to be in charge of your life, the Holy Spirit instantly comes alongside you to be with you as your Best Friend forever. He will guide and direct and keep you. Jesus went to the Jordan River to be baptized by John:

> When Jesus had been baptized and came up immediately from the water . . . behold the heavens were opened to Him and He saw the Spirit of God descending like a dove and alighting upon Him. Suddenly a voice came from heaven saying, "This is My beloved Son in whom I am well pleased."
>
> Matthew 3:16

Jesus had been conceived by the Holy Spirit and yet there was an additional measure, a fullness that came upon Him at His baptism—it was the Holy Spirit in the form of a dove. Jesus was obeying His Father and modeling for us the importance of both water baptism and Holy Spirit baptism. Jesus was the perfect Son of God. He was disciplined and obedient and fulfilled all that had been spoken about Him by centuries of prophetic words recorded in the Bible.

More, Lord

This Holy Spirit experience is available to all of us. If Jesus needed to be baptized in the Holy Spirit, so do you and I. Baptism in the Holy Spirit was never intended to be an addendum to our salvation experience. Every time the apostles preached, we see that they include all three steps—repentance, baptism in water and baptism with the Holy Spirit—in their message.

Immediately after Jesus' water baptism, He was filled with the Holy Spirit (see Luke 4:1). Once He was filled, He was sent into the wilderness to be tested. He passed the test and came out of that experience in the power of the Holy Spirit.

Baptism and continual infilling is how Jesus lived His life as a regular human. The Holy Spirit was His source of power. After the Holy Spirit came upon Jesus, He went everywhere doing good and healing everyone who was being tormented by the devil (see Acts 10:38). The Holy Spirit was with Him just as He wants to be with you.

Jesus spoke to His disciples of two distinct experiences of receiving the Holy Spirit:

> "If you love me, you will obey what I command. And I will ask the Father, and he will give you another Counselor to be with you forever—the Spirit of truth. The world cannot accept him,

because it neither sees him nor knows him. But you know him, for *he lives with you and will be in you.*"

John 14:15–17, NIV, emphasis added

The Holy Spirit already lived "with" them, because they had put their faith in Jesus. Here He was telling them to wait for the Holy Spirit to come be "in" them, which happened at Pentecost. The purpose, they were told, was so that they would be His witnesses in Jerusalem, Judea, Samaria and on to the uttermost parts of the earth. And, indeed, through the infilling of the Holy Spirit at Pentecost, these men and women changed the history of the world.

Not only did those believers have the Holy Spirit come to be "in" them, but they also received a new, supernatural language at the time of their infilling. This wonderful gift, which we will talk more about in chapter 6, was evident every time the baptism of the Holy Spirit is described in the Bible. This language is called "tongues" in Scripture. It is a spiritual language that is deeper than your natural language can ever express. When you do not know what to say, the Holy Spirit does! He will pray through you as you use your supernatural language to communicate with the Father (see Romans 8:27).

CHARGE YOUR BATTERIES

Once you experience this baptism with the Holy Spirit, further infilling is something you can ask for over and over again. Why be "refilled"? Well, we get leaky!

Think of it like a battery. I, Mahesh, received a new iPhone as a gift. I love it, especially as I am often traveling. No matter where I am, as long as I have phone service, I am able to make calls, check my email, surf the web, take notes, even read my Bible!

But no matter how great the phone, after several hours of use it will be completely useless. Why? The battery needs to be recharged. There is nothing wrong with the phone, but it needs to be plugged in.

Life is like that. We find that when we are down to 15 percent charge, we may start griping. At 11 percent we practically start throwing things. At 0 percent, it is hard to remember that we are Christian!

Someone cuts us off on the road and we invent new names for him. Then we think, *Lord, I am saved, but some parts of me are more saved than others!*

The thing is, we have not lost our salvation; we need a change.

The Holy Spirit will help us in weakness (see Romans 8:26). He will recharge our spiritual, emotional and even physical batteries. He gives us strength for living hour by hour and season to season. We are not designed to function without the fullness of the Holy Spirit.

There is no limit to how much we can charge our batteries. His filling does not stop at a set 100 percent. It gets greater and greater. It goes from faith to faith and glory to glory. The level can keep increasing.

Peter's shadow could heal people. Why? His charge kept increasing and increasing. This is true for the Church, too. It is not just about how much "charge" we have individually; it is the collective charge of all of us together that will give us greater influence in our culture.

The essential first step to your relationship with the Holy Spirit comes at salvation. But it is just the beginning of the wonderful friendship He intends to have with you through the infilling of His Spirit.

If you have been baptized with the Holy Spirit, you have received the Holy Spirit. He is not only with you, but in you. If you would like the further infilling of the Holy Spirit, this is available to you right now as well.

There was a time that Peter and John were being persecuted for their faith. They had been arrested and put on trial for healing a man. They prayed for boldness to speak the Word of God, asking that God continue moving with the signs and wonders they performed in the name of Jesus.

Peter and John got with other believers, and when they prayed, the place where they were was shaken, and they were all filled with the Holy Spirit, and they spoke the Word of God with boldness! (see Acts 4:31).

Now, Peter and John had been filled with the Spirit on the Day of Pentecost. Here they asked for boldness to continue their witness to the world, and they are filled again.

This is the pattern we are to follow. Ephesians 5:18 tells us to "be filled with the Spirit." This is not just a command, it is an essential, continuous experience for all Christians. We cannot help but get drained as we go through life day to day; we need to get charged.

Not only will it keep us filled with joy and peace, but it is for our protection. People who are drained make wrong decisions. They even read God's signals incorrectly. People who have been married for years will suddenly decide they need a divorce. Others may think they need to quit their jobs and move to another state. Never make a major decision when your batteries are low!

How do we stay filled?

1. Get connected. Have you tried to turn on a lamp that was not plugged in? Well, it is the same when you want to charge your spiritual batteries. You have to be plugged in. What is our

connection? The heavenly Father. How do we get plugged in? First, salvation through Jesus Christ. Second, baptism in water. Third, baptism with the Holy Spirit. Fourth, joining the fellowship of a local church. When you initially check to see if you are plugged in, make sure these steps are taken care of.

2. Stay immersed in the Scriptures. Read and meditate on the Bible every day.

3. Pray as the Holy Spirit leads you. Pray according to Scriptures or thoughts the Lord may give you for a situation. Use your "supernatural language." Our prayers can go deeper than any words we know. If you ask, the Holy Spirit will bring this dimension into your prayer life.

4. Offer worship, praise and thanksgiving to God.

5. Pray without ceasing. Keep a continual flow of prayer going in your inner thoughts all the time.

6. Learn to hear and obey the voice of the Holy Spirit. (We will look at this dimension in chapters 4 and 5.)

This New Life Is "Anointed"

The Holy Spirit is always at work. The apostle Paul wrote, from revelation and personal experience, that "all the promises of God in [Jesus Christ] are Yes, and in Him Amen, to the glory of God through us" (2 Corinthians 1:20). This means that the more we enter into the promises of God, the more God is glorified.

God has "given us the Spirit in our hearts as a guarantee" (verse 22). Or, "By his Spirit he has stamped us with his eternal pledge—a sure beginning of what he is destined to complete" (The Message).

If you have asked Jesus to forgive you for the wrong things you have done, God has "stamped" you as His. You belong to God, and

His promises are made a real experience for you through the Holy Spirit.

This also means that you have been set apart for His purposes. In the Old Testament we read that kings and priests were anointed for service. In the New Testament we learn from Peter's first letter that because of Jesus' sacrifice, we are actually "kings and priests" before our living God.

What does that mean for your day-to-day life? It means you have been set apart, consecrated for the purposes of God. You have a destiny. You are a child of God. You are special.

And the One who opens the way, who gives access to the Father and then fulfills all of those promises is the Person of the Holy Spirit. He is always about the work of the Father, and one of His main missions is to come and equip us to do the works of God.

When you welcome the work of the Holy Spirit, good things will begin to blossom and grow in your life. Your heart—in fact, your whole being—can be secure and joyful in a dimension that surpasses mere human comprehension. (In chapter 6 we will look more closely at this good fruit. In chapters 7 and 8 we will explore the companion "gifts" the Holy Spirit gives, and help you identify the gifts you already have.)

GOD CARES FOR US DAILY , THANK YOU JESUS

The nations of the world today seem to be in great confusion. Economies, governmental structures, moral strength are declining every day. All of the nations desperately need the grace and mercy of God.

And so without apology, those of us who lean on Jesus' name, who have followed the biblical injunction to repent, be baptized and receive the Holy Spirit (with ongoing infilling), can proclaim that

Jesus is the way out of darkness and confusion and misery. No one need be lost. God has given us the Holy Spirit, and He will guide our lives like a personal pillar of fire.

It does not matter what life throws at us day by day. We can handle the different challenges because by the grace of God the Holy Spirit is with and in us. This is not some kind of religious exercise we are going through. Our Friend has come. He is the one who has been called alongside, and He will never fail.

Paul wrote that in all trials, troubles and tribulations "we are more than conquerors through Him who loved us" (Romans 8:37). That ability to conquer adversity or evil exists because the Holy Spirit comes in Christ's stead to be with us and in us. He transports both Father and Son to us personally moment by moment. All their love and creative power is working in us via the Holy Spirit.

This is the way to walk in newness of life. As you do you will get to know the Holy Spirit more and more, going on from victory to victory, walking in the fullness and the power of this wonderful Friend.

Prayer

Father God, I believe that Jesus died for my sins. I believe that He was buried and that He was resurrected on the third day. I thank You, Lord, that I'm forgiven. All my sins are washed away. I renounce the kingdom of darkness. I receive the Kingdom of God. I receive You, Jesus, as my Lord, as my Savior, and I ask You now to fill me to overflowing with your Holy Spirit according to Your promise. Fill me now, Lord. Baptize me with Your Holy Spirit. I thank You for this wonderful gift.

Chapter 4

When God Talks, Listen

When God thinks about you He thinks big. He thinks good. He thinks long-term. He thinks happy thoughts.

In the very early days of God's involvement in people's lives, He looked for folks who would hear His voice and believe what He said. They were people of faith and action—people like Enoch and Noah, Abraham and Sarah, Isaac and Jacob. Their faith and humility toward God positioned them for heaven's goodness on earth. It put their entire lineages in line for multiplied favor and riches. Their agreement with God was bigger than the best business arrangement and happier than the most wonderful fairy tale.

Still, that commitment was made with a few individuals and their immediate families with the promise of something more: God promised that through Abraham and his progeny, a special people would be given a special land for their own inheritance where they would be planted to grow like a flourishing vine forever.

So, next, God began to multiply His blessing to include more and more people in direct relationship with Him. He began to deal with Israel as a collective nation. He chose a man named Moses to pick up His promise that the whole nation would be His special treasure.

In order to get the children of Israel to that place, He brought them out of slavery and gave them some simple guidelines to follow in order to walk in His provision, protection and blessing every day. These were the Ten Commandments.

Actually God gave Moses ten words from out of His glory when they met on Mount Sinai. Each one carried a whole body of moral clarity and order for the new society being formed. God sent blessing on every aspect of that nation's national, economic and cultural life.

God's plan was that this covenant would create a clear distinction between the people who heard His voice and those who did not, in order that those who did not know Him might choose to do so as they encountered Israel.

The rest of the nations worshiped all sorts of things; they did not know the Living God. So Israel was given a Tabernacle—a tent—in which to worship, and a priesthood was set apart to make regular sacrifices to help His people remember their covenant and keep the relationship between God and His new nation in good standing.

And God did not stop even there. The payoff for His special, chosen people was wave after wave of bigger and better blessing for more and more people until the whole world was included when God sent His Son to save it.

That brings us to the last and final move of God within the human race: It is that of the risen Christ and the Gospel. This is the time (or epoch or "dispensation") humanity is in now.

It began with Jesus' death, burial, resurrection and ascension, and will continue until He comes back, physically, in great glory. At that point, time as we know it will cease to exist. All who have honored Jesus as their Savior and entered into relationship with God through Him will enter their own promised land of eternal life. Magnificent, glorious things that no person has ever imagined await us!

And you can take the first steps onto your promised-land property right now by learning to hear God's voice and to obey. Those are the two conditions that have remained the same in each time period of human history.

God wants you to experience His best life for you now. The key is hearing His voice. And we hear Him speak through the Holy Spirit. In the next chapter, we will discuss obedience to what we have heard.

"GOD-SPEAK"

The Holy Spirit communicates in innumerable ways. Sometimes you will get a mental impression that will seem like your imagination. A sense of direction or a sense of something good coming or a sense of caution about something you are involved in drifts through your mind.

Sometimes it can be a physical sensation in the pit of your stomach, either a joyful sense or a cautionary sense.

Coincidences can be His voice.

He might magnify the words of another person to enter your hearing in a special way, and then you realize that it is actually the Lord using that person's words and voice to speak to you in answer to a prayer or encouragement or insight into a situation.

Sometimes hearing His voice can be as unusual as driving down a highway and having the words on a billboard jump out at you. You recognize that those words are speaking to you about your life or the season you are in.

He often speaks through the Bible. A verse will seem to be lit up on the page, and it will apply to your situation.

Occasionally you might hear the Holy Spirit speak audibly, or it will be so clear it is as though someone were standing by you and speaking clearly.

In a time of great personal need, I, Bonnie, heard, though not with an audible voice, these words very clearly: *You will have a son. Name him Aaron, for I am going to make the rod that is his life bud like Aaron of old.*

I knew there was a story in the Bible where God turned a lifeless stick into the living branch of an almond tree simply from being placed in His Living Presence.

At the time these words came to me, we were expecting our fourth child. I had a severe case of *placenta previa centralis* with hemorrhaging and life-threatening complications. Additionally, I was on complete bed rest.

In the 23rd week my water broke. The placenta broke apart and some of it even fell out of my body. There was no sign of life in my womb, and yet it was then, in those impossible natural circumstances, that the God of impossibility let us know what He was going to do.

And He did it. Today, that child, a son named Aaron, is alive, healthy, handsome, a graduate student who loves God and loves life.

When the Holy Spirit speaks, we can be sure He will do what He said.

Voice-Activated

Voice-activated technology is growing rapidly. Primarily for convenience and for matters of security, everything from computers to bank vaults has voice-activated systems that are designed to recognize the particular sounds of those who are approved for access.

Think of your heart as your personal safe that opens only to one voice, the voice of the Holy Spirit. He will never harm, disappoint or deceive you. You can depend on Him, and this only underlines the importance of learning His voice. As David said in our 23rd Psalm, "The LORD is my shepherd. I shall not want for anything else."

Voices are unique to persons. Nothing in nature has been given as specific a voice as humans have. Why is that? It is because God intends to have a special relationship with us, and He created voice to help that.

This is different from speech: Your voice does not have to make a physical sound to be fully active. Voice is an instrument primarily of the heart. The mouth is secondary. We speak and God hears our hearts. God speaks and we hear Him in our hearts. If sound comes to our physical ears, great! But we need not wait for our ears to hear.

It's Personal

A voice is the expression of personality. No two voices are exactly alike. Jesus said His sheep recognize Him by His voice, and they will not follow a stranger. Our protection, our personal security in receiving guidance and counsel for our lives is hearing His voice.

When it comes to God's voice think of talking to someone on the phone. If you know a person well, or have had a great deal of phone contact, you know who it is immediately without the person having to tell you. When one of your children or your best friend calls you know who it is the instant you hear the sound that is uniquely theirs. You respond entirely differently, usually with reserve, when someone you know less well or a stranger calls.

It is much the same with hearing God. We stay in contact and cultivate our personal relationship with Him, and then when He speaks we welcome His voice.

It's Now!

A voice is always *now* when it is speaking. It speaks in the present. How magnificent to realize that God speaks directly to us, person to person! And as we hear Him, we are relating to the eternal One right now.

God speaks in the eternal realm of faith. That is the way He created everything—except humans! He reached down with His hands and made us out of the dust of the earth.

We need to develop our senses in order to perceive things beyond the physical and into the realm of faith. The Bible says faith is the substance of things we expect from God. It is the evidence of things we cannot see with our natural eyes (see Hebrews 11:1). We apprehend God's voice with our hearts.

When God appeared to Moses in the burning bush and sent him to deliver the children of Israel from slavery, He said, "I AM WHO I AM. Tell them I AM has sent you" (see Exodus 3:14). You can remember something from the past or think of it in the future, but when a voice is speaking it speaks now.

SEVEN KEYS TO HEARING NOW

Since we "hear" the Holy Spirit with our hearts, we need hearts that are in good condition. The steps to keeping our hearts in good condition are not difficult, though they take discipline. Here are seven.

1. Be humble. The wisest (and the richest) man in history, King Solomon, asked God to give him "a hearing heart." Humility means to bow. Humility is the doorman for nearly every other blessing God has for us. The Holy Spirit is called "the Spirit of grace"

(Hebrews 10:29) so everything that involves Him, His Presence, blessing and gifts begins and ends with grace. The humble heart receives grace from God. We need His grace every day.

2. Get personal. Our hearts have "eyes" that enable us to see light. There is one source of the true light that we must have in our hearts in order to see and so hear God. You must make it personal by asking Jesus to come into your heart and cleanse you of your sins. When you have done that, your heart is open to God's voice and ready to obey. Cultivating a sensitive heart begins now, and it is important because sometimes God speaks in gentle whispers. He is not timid—He is God almighty! He does not have to shout to get His point across.

3. Ask! The Lord says that everyone who asks receives (see Luke 11:9–10).

4. "Listen, listening." This odd term is the unique way God describes how we are to regard His voice as He speaks to us. He wants us to hear Him—and to get it! That is because He also expects us to follow through. Obedience, in turn, brings miracles and blessings on you and on your household, family, church, city and nation.

   "If you diligently heed [listen, listening to] the voice of the LORD your God and do what is right in His sight, give ear to His commandments and keep all His statutes, I will put none of these diseases on you which I have brought on the Egyptians. For I am the LORD who heals you" (Exodus 15:26).

   What is the primary requirement? We have to listen to God's voice with all our might; that is to listen, listening. And if we do, God promises that He will accept responsibility for our physical well-being. That is health care! Healing is just one of the multitudes of blessings we receive from hearing and obeying the voice of the Lord.

5. Pay attention. Stand at attention as a soldier ready to receive commands from the general, or as a servant ready to obey his master. Proverbs 4:20 says, "My son, give attention to my words; incline your ear to my sayings." Incline means "to bow."

Everything else you hear (and ultimately think) comes second to what God says. No more unbelief. No more arguments. No more fear. No more telling Him what to do or how to do it. Proverbs 22:17 says, "Incline your ear and hear the words of the wise, and apply your heart to my knowledge." Your heart hears the voice of God as you bow and focus your attention on Him.

People these days are afraid of silence. We have headphones over our ears, while sitting at the computer with the television going in the background just so we don't miss anything that could be happening. Oh, and of course the cell phone is at hand in case somebody calls. The only call we are likely to miss in the midst of all that sensory overload is God's.

Start today observing the number of distractions constantly coming at you. If you really want to focus both ears on Him you will have to get quiet and pay attention to one thing, one Person, at a time.

6. Be ready to learn. Mr. Humility is holding the door of your heart open; you will enter God's classroom. You are not there to instruct Him; it is the other way around. The Holy Spirit is called the teacher. He wants to impart God's wisdom and knowledge without holding anything back.

   Remember the kid in class who was the know-it-all? Nobody likes a know-it-all. That kind of person keeps everyone else from learning and never learns the important things for himself. Our own preconceptions, prejudices and ideas, even religious dogma, can make us deaf when it comes to hearing God.

7. Be still. Psalm 46:10 says, "Be still, and know that I am God." Cease striving. Let go. Relax.

   King David was a man with a heart after God. He learned to wait quietly for God to speak to him. In one of his psalms he wrote: "My soul, wait in silence for God alone" (Psalm 62:5). David took command of his concerns needing to be worked through, national decisions needing to be made, battles needing to be won and kings needing to be subdued and said, "My soul waits in silence for God only."

Was That You, God?

Faith is a vital part of hearing God: The more you begin to hear and respond, the more you will learn to recognize His voice and understand His particular way of speaking to you. His language is very personal, and you will find that the more you get to know His voice, the more you will realize He will speak to you in a language that is unique to you.

God would regularly tell His servants to go to a certain place, and when they arrived what they observed was a living parable of God's message to His people.

He told Jeremiah, for instance, "Go down to the potter's house. I have something I want to tell you." Jeremiah got there and saw the potter working the clay on his wheel. The voice of the Lord gave Jeremiah a message for God's people illustrating the fact that we are clay in the Master Potter's hands being formed into vessels He is ordaining and designing.

Because dialogue with God is mostly internal, His voice will often sound just like your own voice, as though the word is your own thought. Maybe you are a nurse: You will find that He uses medical terminology. Maybe you are a writer or a pet sitter: The terms He uses might have to do with your craft.

When you are making a decision it is good to have more than one confirmation. Here are reliable ways to verify whether or not what you are hearing is from the Lord.

Your Operator's Manual

The Bible is a supernatural book, and that means He will make the words come alive for you every day as advice and strength and encouragement.

The year when I, Bonnie, was finishing high school one of my teachers asked me if I would like to spend the summer in New York working in her restaurant.

I thought that sounded exciting and accepted the offer. I soon befriended some of the other girls who worked there, but was horrified to learn that one of them was a member of a violent biker gang. I learned further that the gang members had their eyes on me to induct me into their world. This was very frightening because I saw no way out.

As a child I had thanked Jesus for being my Savior and asked Him to be the Lord over every part of my life. I had been taught that I could lean on what the Bible said, but I had no idea what exactly that was. I had never studied His Word as a child, and now in my teens, I had turned from the closeness I once had with God.

My mother had given me a translation called the Living Bible, and for some unknown reason I had taken it with me, but I had no idea of the content. It was just a big thick book with a bunch of pages and a bunch of words starting at Genesis and going all the way to Revelation.

But I knew that somewhere in that book were specific things that held authority and wisdom to help me when I did not have a human friend or a defender.

So I remember I picked up that Living Bible, which I had not cracked open since she gave it to me, and sort of thumbed through it trying to find some kind of defense. I said, "Lord, I need some way to explain to these gang members that I want to be left alone."

That night when I was at work I recognized a man who was part of a large church campground just up the road from us. The campground hosted large gatherings of people who wanted to learn more about the Bible. It was quite vibrant and famous in that area.

When I saw that gentleman from the campground I felt very excited. I wrote him a little note on a restaurant napkin asking if I might speak with him for a moment after he had finished with his dinner. He waited for me as we waitresses wrapped up the dinner service. I went over to his table, introduced myself, sat down and told him what was going on.

This man appeared to be absolutely terrified for me. He shared Scriptures with me, but he could not help but ask, "What were you thinking?" And he was right. By developing those dangerous friendships I was not following in the path the Lord desired for me.

My ordeal came to a showdown with the gang leader and other members, and I used the words of Scripture that the gentleman had showed me in the Bible to rebuff their threats.

To this day I cannot tell you why they backed off from me, except to say that the Holy Spirit had never left me from the time I had come to Him as a child. Even though I had made bad decisions as a young adult, I learned that there was an invisible Person there with me all the time. When I called out to God, He was more than ready to help me.

Scripture lays down basic principles to guide and instruct us. It also demonstrates how God goes about His business. Here then is the vital question: Do the words we think God has spoken to us agree with the example, direction and substance of what the Bible says?

This is of utmost importance.

"All Scripture is given by inspiration of God, and is profitable for doctrine, for reproof, for correction, for instruction in righteousness" (2 Timothy 3:16).

Inspired means the Holy Spirit has breathed into the Word that has been written and preserved for us. Second Peter 1:20–21 says, "No prophecy of Scripture . . . came by the will of man, but holy men of God spoke as they were moved by the Holy Spirit." All the humans involved in writing down the Bible were carried along by

Someone Divine: the Holy Spirit. He will never say something that does not agree with His Word.

To be sure you have heard His voice, check it against what the Bible says. Do the two agree?

If the voice you heard does not line up with Scripture, it may be a counterfeit. Get quiet and wait for the Lord to speak. He will speak what is right.

Road Signs

A couple who works in the banking industry shared with us how God used literal road signs to confirm His direction for them:

Jack and Sue had been praying about some major decisions that would affect their job and their family and would give them a new season in their life. As they prayed, they felt they had gotten direction from the Lord, but it would require them to take a big step of faith. Later that week they made a road trip and were discussing what they felt God was encouraging them to do. At every juncture in their conversation, they would look up and see a road sign echoing exactly what they felt the Lord was telling them! The first sign simply said in big letters, "Second Chance." A few mintues later there was a billboard for a national bank that had the slogan "Family First." And finally, they passed a sign that simply said, "Got Faith?"

Coincidence? We don't think so. This is how wonderful the Holy Spirit is. He is personal and knows exactly what we need and how we need to hear it. He can use even our natural surroundings to catch our attention and put an exclamation point on what He has already whispered in our ear when we have sought His direction and guidance.

From large-scale direction for whole nations to personal affirmation on an individual level, the Holy Spirit often speaks through natural circumstances. The Bible is full of examples where certain natural events have a spiritual connotation. Drought, for instance, is often a physical indication of the spiritual condition of the land.

In the book of Joel we read how the land was completely ravished by drought and swarms of locusts. There was nothing but misery and despair. But then, as the people turned back to God, He answered in the spiritual realm (by promising to bless the land, animals and people) and the natural realm (by rainfall). Gloom and despair were washed away. The land grew fruitful and was restored from all the devastation.

For several years many regions of the United States were suffering from extreme drought conditions. Lakes, rivers and reservoirs were drying up. But then, suddenly, the Lord poured out rain. The reservoirs became full to overflowing.

As we witnessed the rains coming down in parts of the United States after the terrible drought, a number of us who worship together believed that we heard the Lord say, *The drought is over!*

We believed that in this case there was a spiritual message for us that paralleled the natural event. We understood God to be saying that *drought* had been affecting more than land; it had been affecting many of our lives with barrenness and deadness in various areas, whether the ability to reach people with the Good News of Jesus or finances or productivity or any number of other things as well.

Believing that we had heard the Holy Spirit directing us to pray about this, we asked God to break the drought over our lives and send His wonderful refreshing rain of blessing on us and our children, just as He was sending the earth-quenching rain over the land.

Generally, when the Holy Spirit speaks through natural circumstances the confirmations are very personal.

Suppose you have felt that the Lord wants you to do something special for another person, but you realize you do not have the resources you need. After praying about it you unexpectedly receive the supply for what you felt you were to do. That is your go-ahead.

The Bible has lots of examples of people asking for a sign to know that what they were hearing was from God. Gideon is a famous example.

An angel appeared to Gideon with a message that the Lord was calling him to rise up and lead Israel into battle against an enemy that was invading and pillaging their land. Gideon asked for a sign. During the night God caused exactly what Gideon asked for to occur. So Gideon prepared for action and called people together.

Before risking those people's lives, Gideon wanted to be very sure he had indeed heard from the Lord and that God was with them for success. Gideon asked for a new sign. In fact, he asked for a third sign. He said, "Lord, forgive me if I'm insisting on being sure it's You, but could You confirm it again by such and such?"

When morning came and God had given him the third sign, Gideon flew into action full of faith and with the power of the Holy Spirit on him and on those who went with him.

In another instance God told a king to ask for a miraculous sign, but the king refused. God was very displeased with the king's reluctance to ask for a sign, and gave the king a sign Himself.

We do offer one word of caution on demanding signs. Asking for a sign again and again without ever acting on what God has said to do can be a problem of unbelief or fear or some other obstacle you need to deal with.

And being solely dependent on God showing you a sign before you obey becomes childish after a while. God wants mature sons and daughters who are walking in the kind of relationship with Him in which they easily recognize His voice and know the proper manner in which to obey.

Two or Three Others

> It is like the precious oil upon the head, running down on the beard, the beard of Aaron, running down on the edge of his garments. It is like the dew of Hermon, descending upon the mountains of Zion; for there the Lord commanded the blessing— life forevermore.
>
> Psalm 133:2–3

Jesus sits as Head over His Body of believers. The Holy Spirit flows from Him like oil all the way down to us, bringing blessing.

God joins us with people who can affirm what He is speaking. Every relationship in a godly community is an asset for hearing Him.

A woman in our church was seeking the Lord about expanding her business. After several days of prayer and fasting she felt the Holy Spirit was speaking a particular Scripture to her from the story of Isaac digging wells for his flocks. That same day, another member of our church who knew nothing of her situation emailed her, saying, "I've had you on my heart all day today. I was praying for you and felt the Lord gave me this Scripture for you." It was the Scripture she had just gotten from the Lord. Needless to say, she felt confident that she was hearing from the Lord and moving in the right direction!

God places people in authority in our lives. The Bible is clear about the sanctity of certain relationships, among them marriage, giving each spouse certain rights and responsibilities, such as the husband in headship of the home. Similarly, parents stand in authority over their children, and pastors are given charge over their flocks. Godly authority is meant to be a safeguard and a blessing. If we respect and honor it, God will respect and honor us, too.

We have seen some crazy things, like people deciding they should get a divorce or marry someone else because of a "word" they heard from the Lord. If you are entering a situation where the ethical or moral rules of Scripture—and especially God's basic commandments—are being violated, do not proceed. Seek the counsel of your pastor or the person who has ongoing spiritual oversight and input with authority in your life.

If you do not have a person like that whom you can trust to give you godly counsel, finding one is the first step in getting you into a place where you can learn to hear God's voice and receive His blessings. We live in a culture that worships independence and individualism of every kind. "If it feels good do it" is not a good rule of thumb when it comes to receiving heaven's blessing. Seek out trustworthy leaders who can help you.

There is an example of help that can come when we are in unity in Acts 13:1–3. Members of the church in Antioch were together worshiping the Lord and seeking His direction. They all heard the voice of the Holy Spirit saying, "Now separate to Me Barnabas and Saul [who became Paul] for the work to which I have called them." They fasted and prayed together, and then they placed their hands on the two men and sent them off.

This was the assurance for Barnabas and Paul, through their brothers in the assembly, that the call they heard was from God. The Holy Spirit was giving, through their fellow believers, a witness that their direction was right. And the fellowship further joined them in faith for strength and support as they obeyed.

This incident emphasizes the interdependence of the members of Christ's Body. God created us to live in communities of special ongoing relationship with others. His spiritual gifts particularly demonstrate and emphasize this fact. We need one another to get the full benefit, blessing and picture of what God is doing and saying. We need others participating with us in our lives and they need us, too!

Peace in Your Heart

> Let the peace of God rule in your hearts, to which also you were called in one body; and be thankful. Let the word of Christ dwell in you richly in all wisdom, teaching and admonishing one another in psalms and hymns and spiritual songs, singing with grace in your hearts to the Lord.
>
> Colossians 3:15–16

Remember that hearing begins in your heart. That is where Christ's spiritual heavenly throne is built on earth. Peace in your heart means the King is on His throne. You can move ahead with assurance.

Think about an umpire at a baseball game calling a player "safe" or "out." He knows the rules. He watched the play. He has the authority to make the call.

Peace from Jesus is the "call" that determines whether or not what you heard is from God. His peace says, *Yes.* If you have no peace, be cautious. If pressure and unrest are coming from what you have heard, be on your guard and do not act hastily. It could mean that you are not hearing right or that you are not applying what you heard correctly or it is not the right time. The *when* is as important as the *what, how, where* and *who.*

Peace brings thankfulness with it. So if it is easy to praise the Lord and thank Him as you go about obeying, you are probably on the right track.

There is ease that comes from His presence. There is joy that comes as we rest in Him. You will find that you begin to excel in all that you do because your thoughts are directed by His wisdom and voice. God intends for the people who know His voice to work smarter, not necessarily harder.

Now let's move to the next part of hearing God's voice. After we listen, we must obey. This is the subject of the next chapter.

Prayer

Thank You, Lord, that Your Holy Spirit dwells inside me. I forgive all those who have hurt or harmed me. Cleanse me, Lord, from any pride, resentment, anger or any unclean thing. My heart is open to hear the still small voice of Your Spirit. Thank You for drawing me closer to You.

Chapter 5

BLESSINGS

Several years ago I, Mahesh, was in the middle of an intense ministry schedule. I had a layover in Chicago, and I was so tired I fell asleep while waiting for my next flight. I almost missed my plane, except I heard the Lord speak to me: *Wake up, sleeping beauty!*

Glad to be boarding the plane, I remember thinking, *The Lord has never called me sleeping beauty before!* I went on with my commitments and came home to Charlotte late Saturday night, exhausted and ready just to fall into bed.

Unbeknownst to me, Bonnie had received an urgent phone call from some dear friends in Nashville. Lynn, the lead guitarist of a country music band, was in a diabetic coma. She had been unconscious for several hours before she was found and rushed to the hospital.

Doctors had little hope for her survival. A blood sugar level of 180 is considered to be the high end of normal. Lynn's blood sugar had spiked to 1966! The sugar had crystallized in her blood vessels and caused irreversible damage to the delicate tissues of her brain, nerves and internal organs. Her organs were shutting down and there was really little hope for her outside of a miracle.

Bonnie told all of this to me as I was walking in from the airport late in the evening. My heart went out to my friends in this hopeless situation, but my body and mind were drained of virtue. I could not imagine heading right back out the door to travel to Nashville where Lynn was in the hospital.

The next morning I was ministering Holy Communion when the Lord spoke the same words into my heart that I had heard in Chicago: *Wake up, sleeping beauty.*

Suddenly I realized those words were not for me: He was giving me a word from His heart for the woman who lay in the hospital in Nashville. God was telling me to go pray for her healing. Immediately after the service I left for the hospital in Nashville with two men from our church.

As we entered the intensive care ward, I found that Lynn was barely hanging on to life. All of her vital organs were shutting down. The doctors said that the neurological damage she had suffered was irreversible. This talented musician, if she survived, would lose her sight and all her fine motor skills.

But there was another reality in the room. It seemed as if so many angels were attending us on this mission that there was hardly room for people to surround her bed. I felt the presence of God with us for healing as we anointed Lynn with oil and I spoke the word that God had given me for her that morning. I knew God wanted her to live and not die. So now all waited for Him to show His glory.

God woke up that sleeping beauty and healed her completely. Within three days Lynn walked out of the hospital under her own steam completely restored to health. In fact Lynn pushed the attending nurse to the door in the wheelchair Lynn was to have been escorted in!

God wants to train you in this hour to be someone who hears the voice of the Holy Spirit and obeys. As you learn to recognize and respond to His voice, you will be able to see His reality and not feel thwarted by any circumstances around you.

The twelve spies that Moses sent into the Promised Land are a good example of this. Ten spies came back with a bad report of giants, fortified cities and the impossibility of the situation. Two spies, Joshua and Caleb, came back ready to take the land God had promised.

Joshua and Caleb were of a different spirit. They were not basing their decision on what they saw with their eyes, but were responding to what the Lord had spoken to Moses and all of Israel.

The Holy Spirit is the inheritance that God has promised to all of us beginning with Pentecost. He gave us the gift of His Spirit to speak to us, encourage us, direct us and instruct us so we can hear and obey. Obedience is the way to see His miracles displayed.

RECEIVE YOUR BLESSINGS

Have you ever worried about some kind of misfortune catching up with you and wrecking some area of your life?

You can make sure the very opposite happens by learning to work with God as He speaks to you. Deuteronomy 28:2 says that God has commanded *blessings* to catch up to you and overtake you! The Bible then names 26 categories of blessings we all can receive, covering everything from our paychecks to our pets.

God wants us to be dynamic and victorious people. If we are willing to listen and obey, we can be sure we will see the great power of His hand at work around us.

Here are just three examples of blessings that can be ours when we fulfill these two directives.

Bless Your Children

Deuteronomy 28:4 says that our children and other areas of "increase" will be blessed: "Blessed shall be the fruit of your body, the produce of your ground and the increase of your herds, the increase of your cattle and the offspring of your flocks."

If you are raising children, do you realize you need the voice of the Lord every day? There have been times when we have thought, *Why didn't I get training? I should have waited until I was older and wiser. I have no idea what to do!*

But the Lord is with you. He will speak to you, and as you raise them, being guided by the voice of the Lord, they will be blessed. The added blessing comes as you train your children to hear the voice of the Lord. Then they will also walk in the blessing of God as they grow and have families of their own.

Bless Your Work

Deuteronomy 28:5 says: "Blessed shall be your basket and your kneading bowl."

Your "basket" represents your work, your business, your place of employment. As you hear and obey the voice of the Lord, your work will be blessed.

God loves you and wants to bless you in every area of your life and work. As you relate to the Holy Spirit, He will help you set priorities even in mundane tasks.

Are you a "list" person? Lists are very helpful for staying on track and being attentive to what needs to be done. But how many times have you looked at your list and been overwhelmed? Or have gotten bogged down in a project and later realized you had three other tasks that were more critical that now are behind schedule?

As God blesses your work, He will even help you to make lists and will sanctify your lists so that His wisdom and direction begin to influence how you prioritize and approach your work.

Your cup can be overflowing with abundance. You can be prosperous and debt-free. He will give you the principles you need to guide and instruct you.

Blessed Victory

Deuteronomy 28:7 says: "The LORD will cause your enemies who rise against you to be defeated before your face; they shall come out against you one way and flee before you seven ways."

The voice of the Lord will give you victory over your enemies. In the natural realm many nations face threats of various kinds, but God is talking here about our spiritual enemies. The devil walks about, 1 Peter 5:8 says, like a roaring lion seeking someone to devour.

Today, what are your enemies? Fear? Oppression? Lack? Division?

God does not guarantee that there will not be attacks, but He does promise that He will defeat every enemy that comes against you.

THE RIGHT ATTITUDE

These are just a few of the blessings we are promised. Note that this is not a matter of wanting something and "claiming" or declaring it to be yours simply because you want it. This is a journey. You are walking day by day, choosing to learn to listen and to obey. But you are not alone. The Holy Spirit is right there with you. He is not only directing you, but He is filling you with the power and the desire to take the path of obedience that brings blessings and more blessings to you, God's son or daughter.

Blessed Sons and Daughters

Have you seen a freshly pruned tree? It is not a pretty sight. It often looks more as though its legs and arms have been amputated.

But as we know, the cutting process causes the tree to create new growth that is stronger and loaded with more fruit-bearing potential than before.

If you feel as though His gardening shears are being applied to your branches, be encouraged. Jesus said, "I am the Vine and you are My branches and My Father is the Orchard Keeper who comes to prune and tend the vines" (see John 15). In God's eyes that means you are a real son or daughter. God "legitimizes" our adoption through discipline, challenge, correction and difficulty. Even Jesus was "proved" in the way metal is refined.

> "My son, do not make light of the Lord's discipline, and do not lose heart when he rebukes you, because the Lord disciplines those he loves, and he punishes everyone he accepts as a son." Endure hardship as discipline; God is treating you as sons. For what son is not disciplined by his father? . . . God disciplines us for our good, that we may share in his holiness.
>
> Hebrews 12:5–7, 10, NIV

When was the last time you heard someone refer to discipline as love? We live in a lawless and loveless culture. Jesus wants us to experience something different. He sends His Spirit to bring that experience to us. Realize:

> No discipline seems pleasant at the time, but painful. Later on, however, it produces a harvest of righteousness and peace for

those who have been trained by it. Therefore, strengthen your feeble arms and weak knees.

Hebrews 12:11–12, NIV

There is a desperate need for people to discover they become real sons and daughters of God when they are born again. People need to know who they are. You need to know. You need to know you are not an orphan. You need to know you are not without "parents" who love you. The Father, Son and Spirit have adopted you if you have received Christ as your Savior.

When we realize this we view life through a very different lens. We realize that God has eternity in mind for us, and He deals with us as His own children. Paul tells us that our goal as Christians is to come "to the measure of the stature of the *fullness* of Christ" and to "grow up in all things into Him" (Ephesians 4:13, 15, emphasis added).

A woman named Katherine told us how this knowledge changed her.

> God has changed me. Depression and anxiety are gone and my faith is more real to me. This has only continued to grow. My whole approach to my life is changed from self-centered to Christ-centered. I am not discouraged or shamed by my shortcomings. Relationships that I wanted to avoid, I now want to seek out so that I can love the people because I see how much God loves them. I want to sacrifice what I need to in order to obey Christ and let Him touch others. I want God to receive glory for His greatness and goodness. I have confidence that I am right where God has put me and I will continue to be positioned by Him. I know I have a great future.

The Holy Spirit is the One who gracefully sends conviction on our hearts to turn us to God. Jesus said the Holy Spirit would do three important things. First, He would minister conviction of sin. Where we miss the mark by not believing the truth about Jesus, He comes to lead us into light. And as we turn and exercise more and more faith He continues to help us grow.

Second, He would lead us in the right way of thinking and moral living. We need to have Jesus' example made real to us day by day in order to live a successful life.

And third, He would administer judgment. People avoid the very word. But we cannot have truth without judgment; we cannot distinguish good from evil, right from wrong.

Without truth we are left alone in spiritual darkness. The Holy Spirit is the agent through whom the right way is communicated to us. When Jesus comes again, He is coming for those who are walking with Him in His light.

Recently I, Bonnie, was reminded of how much this life of obedience is a step-by-step process. I was upset by the actions of someone who spoiled something I took great pleasure in. As I sat there looking at what had been done, my frustration and anger kept rising.

It dimmed my inner lights and took away my joy. I felt as though I were being dragged deeper and deeper into a dark pit. I cried out to the Lord just as I was about to be overcome. I could sense that the longer I let anger have its way, the longer it would take to restore my peace and joy.

Realizing the Holy Spirit knew what I really needed at the moment, I asked Him to guide my prayers. I got hold of my thoughts and turned them to the realization of how much my sin had spoiled Jesus' glory and ruined His body as He gave Himself away for me on the cross. I thought how petty my present disappointment was in comparison, and how temporary when compared to what He has gained for me eternally.

I repented.

In a little while, as I persisted in giving myself to the Spirit, keeping my eyes on Jesus, fresh streams from His Presence began slowly to trickle into the pooling frustration in my heart. After some more time pursuing His grace, forgiveness and peace, the release from the pit began to come. My joy along with love for "the spoiler" returned.

The Holy Spirit is the Chief Construction Agent assigned to oversee God's building project: us! He is making each of us who get to know Him into an ever more glorious dwelling place. Let's not miss out on a single thing!

Can you see His pruning as a measure of His love? Seek victory more than escape and rejoice when escape comes, for, the truth is, the process has changed you for the better.

OVERCOMING

There are many examples in the Bible of people walking in obedience and seeing the rewards the Holy Spirit brought into their lives.

The first one whose work is mentioned in relation to the Holy Spirit is called Bezalel. The Holy Spirit gave him the ability to envision, design and craft the precious vessels used in the Tabernacle. Craftsmanship like his had never been seen before.

Joshua became a great military leader who conquered the enemies in the Promised Land. A young man named Gideon led Israel to defeat a multitude that had threatened Israel's safety and had been robbing them blind season after season. Noah built a huge boat in the middle of a desert. Moses chopped down a tree and threw it in a poisoned lake, and it made the water drinkable and life-giving.

These persons all started out in their own strength and their own state of mind. And then God came in power and anointed them with

Himself! When they obeyed Him, they went from weak to strong, from afraid to fearless, from overcome to overcomers.

They heard and obeyed. You can, too.

God made you. He wrote the operation manual for how you will best flourish for living. Why not take a leap of faith and trust that our Father knows best? The trade-off for obedience is that "all these blessings" will overtake you.

When we walk according to the leading of the Holy Spirit we are not always able to see far into the distance. That is what makes it a walk of faith. But we can be sure that we will never walk in the dark. There will be enough light to take the next step. So on we go, one step at a time, doing what we have heard and waiting for further leading.

Prayer

Come, Holy Spirit, and fill every empty place in my life. Every place where there is lack. Every place where there has been defeat. Every place where I need Your overcoming power and blessing. Come and transform me from the inside out. Father God, You know what is best for my life, and desire to give good gifts to Your children. Help me to hear Your voice and obey the leading of Your Holy Spirit so that I and my family can more fully enjoy the blessings that come from following Jesus Christ.

Chapter 6

FLOURISH

As we become closer friends with the Holy Spirit, we see that His work involves a wonderful plan and purpose for us. When we respond, He helps us become more like Jesus. Fruit of the Spirit and gifts of the Spirit in our lives are evidence that He is present and working.

THE DIFFERENCE BETWEEN FRUIT AND GIFTS

Nine types of fruit of the Spirit are listed in the Bible. These reveal the divine character of the Holy Spirit. They are love, joy, peace, patience, kindness, goodness, faithfulness, gentleness, self-control.

Complementing the fruit are the numerous supernatural gifts. The gifts the Spirit gives indicate His divine ability, things like wisdom, faith and healing. (We will study these in the next two chapters.)

Jesus manifested fully and perfectly both the divine *character* of God and the divine *ability* of God. If He had manifested divine character without ability, He could never have healed the sick and freed the oppressed who came to Him in throngs (see Matthew 9:6).

On the other hand, if Jesus had exhibited divine ability without character, He would never have humbled Himself in love and died on the cross in our stead. He could have escaped that torture at any moment. The fruit of love made Him do what He did. Love made Him finish what He started in spite of the cost (see Matthew 26:52–53).

To understand the difference between fruit and gifts we could think of an apple tree. The delicious fruit we eat, make pies out of, make applesauce and apple cider with all begins with a seed. The seed is planted, grows and eventually becomes a tree that produces apples. These apples also have seeds in them that can be used to plant more apple trees that will eventually grow more apples with more seeds.

This is like fruit of the Spirit. Harmony with God through daily personal relationship makes us want to be like Him and helps us do so. We think like Him, we act like Him, we treat others the way He treats us. In other words, because the Holy Spirit indwells us, His character, or fruit, is like a seed that can grow inside us and resemble the tree from which it came.

The gifts of the Spirit are very different. They are the Chinese lanterns hung in the tree branches to adorn it and make it more dramatic, more festive. They are added to the tree; they are not the product of its natural growth. The gifts give us power beyond natural human ability.

We should not confuse the bestowal of gifts as approval of anyone's character, any more than we think receiving a birthday present affirms we are the perfect human being! Spiritual gifts are presents of unmerited divine favor called grace. They indicate God's nature, not His approval of ours.

Gifts are given to every person who receives Christ. God decides which gifts we will get, and even when we falter He never takes them back: "The gifts and calling of God are irrevocable" (Romans 11:29). And sometimes He even blesses things and persons He does not necessarily endorse (see Job 5:10). As we know, when it rains it rains on everybody in the neighborhood, not just the homes of the nice people!

Gifts come instantly; fruit takes time.

THE APPEARANCE OF FRUIT

As the Holy Spirit is in you, the potential is there for the fruit—or the force—of the Spirit to come out—the force of love, the force of joy, the force of peace and so on. It is all there; you just tap into it. The more you release your faith, the more His fruit will be evident in you.

Faith comes by hearing and hearing by the Word of God. So we can hear the Word of God and let faith come. Then when faith comes, the fruit of His character will become evident in us. Love will come by hearing the Word of God. Self-control will come by hearing the Word of God. Kindness will come.

It is when the pressure is on that you realize your faith is taking hold and the fruit of the Holy Spirit is being produced within you.

Take joy, for instance. There is much in the world that would try to steal your joy—the evening news, heavy traffic, loud neighbors, cranky co-workers. That is when your joy acts like the little thruster that puts you into the orbit of faith. You determine that you are not going to be out of touch with your joy. Joy, goodness, kindness, self-control, patience—all of these fruits are protective barriers around you that keep you from fear or depression or anger.

Look at this wonderful verse from the book of Job. You remember about the longsuffering of Job? Everything that could go wrong, went wrong. Job 5:22 says that in destruction and famine you shall (blank).

How would you fill in the blank? In destruction and famine you shall get depressed? In destruction and famine you shall be fearful? In destruction and famine you shall murmur? In destruction and famine you shall complain?

No: "In destruction and famine you shall laugh"! What an amazing thought!

Or maybe it is a time such as the prophet Habakkuk was facing:

> Though the fig tree may not blossom, nor fruit be on the vines, though the labor of the olive may fail, and the fields yield no food; though the flocks may be cut off from the fold, and there be no herd in the stalls . . .

This was a bad time. No fig trees, no olives, the flock is cut off from the fold, no herds—it is another case of destruction and famine. Yet what does the prophet say?

> . . . yet I will rejoice in the Lord, I will joy in the God of my salvation. The Lord God is my strength; He will make my feet like the deer's feet, and He will make me walk on my high hills.

> Habakkuk 3:17–19

That is fruit in a person's life. Everything can be falling apart, but you are not defeated. When you are filled with the Spirit and the fruit is ripe in your life, you are armed with power that can overcome.

And to look at it another way, when people are not joyful (or full of any of the other fruit) they are seldom able to use their faith either.

Bearing Fruit in and out of Season

As we have seen, when we accept Jesus as Savior, the Holy Spirit comes to indwell us. Because He is ever present with us, His fruit—the fruit of a life that honors Jesus—becomes evident. That is, it *should* become evident. The story in the Bible about Jesus and the fig tree gives us good insight into Jesus' expectations of those who bear His name.

Here is the story that Mark tells in his gospel.

> Now the next day, when they had come out from Bethany, [Jesus] was hungry. And seeing from afar a fig tree having leaves, He went to see if perhaps He would find something on it.
>
> Mark 11:12–14

If you are familiar with the story, you know that there were no figs on that tree. You might also remember what Jesus said when He saw it: "In response Jesus said to it, 'Let no one eat fruit from you ever again.' And His disciples heard it" (verse 14).

But before telling us that Jesus cursed the fig tree, Mark gives a catchphrase that puts Jesus' actions in a most peculiar light: "It was not the season for figs" (verse 13).

Now you would think that Jesus—being compassionate and being the Creator and no doubt being earth-friendly!—when He saw that this poor fig tree was just doing what it was supposed to be doing, would have blessed it and said, "I'll come back again in a season when you're supposed to have fruit."

But that is not what He did. Instead He cursed the fig tree. He said, "You don't have figs now, and you'll never have figs again."

In order to get the proper perspective on bearing fruit in our own lives, we need to understand the message that Jesus was giving in this living parable.

STAYING READY

This lesson from the fig tree came at an important point in the timeline of Jesus' life. The previous day was the day of His triumphal entry into Jerusalem, announcing to the world that the Messiah had come; by the end of the week He would be dead. This was His last week on earth. The larger context of this lesson was His future return to earth in His Second Coming.

Through the fig tree Jesus was teaching His disciples—including us—to be ready, for He could return at any time. It might not happen when it is convenient; it might not happen when everything is going right. In fact, it is quite likely that Jesus will come at a moment that is inconvenient for the natural man. It will not be a season when love, joy, peace, patience, kindness, goodness, faithfulness, gentleness and self-control will be the natural state of the world.

As we move closer to the time of His return, we will see greater confusion and chaos socially, politically, economically and spiritually. This is the very reason why being filled with the Holy Spirit, and His fruit and His gifts, is such good news.

God's people will become water in a dry world, or salt to preserve goodness, or lights in a dark place. Your future and the future of your children can be joyfully and securely settled on Someone eternal who has all power, who is working everything in our lives to a grand and beautiful climax of goodness, and most of all who is pure Love.

That One who promised never to leave us is our Friend, the Holy Spirit. The people who know Him will be supernatural people in this natural world.

PRODUCING MORE FRUIT

Furthermore, consider this. When the Holy Spirit helps us produce one kind of fruit, it naturally produces another.

God is love, for instance, and He plants the seed of His supernatural love in each one who knows Him. As we nurture and nourish God's love, we find ourselves more and more in a perpetual joyful state. So love produces the fruit of joy.

Then take peace. God is Jehovah Shalom—the God of peace. As we allow Him to plant the seed of His peace and well-being in us, it grows like a vine and eventually pushes out weeds of insecurity and restlessness. Further, it produces fruit of patience, the ability to wait restfully through difficulty, trusting God's answer to come because He is good.

Or kindness. It is the kindness of God that allows us to experience His goodness. Likewise, when we nurture God's kindness, it causes us to express goodness toward others and, more and more, the atmosphere around us is good!

Psalm 18:35 says, "Your gentleness has made me great." When we think about the example of Jesus' gentleness, we realize that it gave Him the ability to know what to do when. He knew when to speak and when to hold His peace. That is self-control. So the fruit of a gentle spirit strengthens our ability to govern our own otherwise negative emotional actions and reactions.

You could consider all of these partnered in the reverse. If you practice self-control you will become conscious of not treating people harshly. If you practice goodness, you will be aware of being kind to others. If you develop patience you will find yourself able to live at peace. And if you cultivate joy you will find your own heart growing larger and larger in love and grace toward others.

Jesus is the ultimate nurseryman in our orchards. There is a harvest He is looking for. It is the fruit of the Spirit He is cultivating in us. When He comes, He is going to expect something beyond the natural, beyond what we can do with our own strength. That is why the Holy Spirit says, "Not by your power, not by your might, but through Me" (see Zechariah 4:6).

Our job is to stay fruitful until He comes. How do we do this?

OUR SPIRITUAL SACRIFICE

Let's return to the story of the fig tree for a moment. It opens with these words: "But on the following day when they came from Bethany He was hungry."

Did you ever think about that? That God can actually be hungry? We know that He is perfect and complete in Himself, yet Jesus knew hunger, thirst, sorrow and grief. We could take this beyond Jesus' earthly existence and ponder the mystery of why, though complete in Himself, God wanted someone else to love.

God did not create the man and woman in the Garden to worship Him. That was not His motivation. Worship is the supernatural response to the revelation of Himself as a Person. His whole motivation from beginning to end—Jesus' incarnation, the cross, the resurrection and His coming again—His entire motivation is His desire for one-on-one fellowship. He longs to have His family all together as a kind of enrichment in Him, and we are part of that.

He is hungry, and He is hoping that His Body on earth, His Church, will produce fruit. As we fellowship with Him we become like Him, and we do just that. We become trees, like the ones in the book of Revelation, that offer healing and food for the nations.

Our natural strength will not satisfy the Lord when He is hungry. He is looking for something supernatural, and that is not too much to expect, because He did something supernatural at Calvary: He opened the door that gave access to the Spirit that we might become a supernatural race.

The anointing to do great things by faith is inseparable from the fruit of the Spirit. When we pray, we are standing in the authority of Christ. We go about doing great things until He comes again. When He returns, suddenly, He will be looking for those who are bearing fruit. Those who are in Him will be ready.

What Faith Can Do

The next morning, after Jesus spoke to the fig tree, Mark 11 tells us that He and His disciples passed by, and they saw the fig tree "dried up from the roots" (verse 20). Then Peter said something to the effect of: "Wow, I'm shocked! Look, Rabbi! What You said came to pass."

What does Jesus say? "Have faith in God."

Whom is He speaking to here? He is speaking to us, to His disciples. "Truly I say to you, whoever says to this mountain be taken up and thrown into the sea and does not doubt in his heart but believes that what he says will come to pass, it will be done."

How is this possible? Could it be that if you will trust in God with all your heart you can speak something and He will bring it to pass? Yes. We are living branches of the Tree of Life, the fruit of the death, burial and resurrection of the Son of Glory.

This same Spirit that raised Jesus up from the grave comes to reside in everyone who asks Him. That is power for change. That is the realm God calls His glory, which glory He wants to give to those who love Him. The glory is like another dimension; it is a reality that supersedes nature's laws. In the realm of the Spirit's glory, things that have been bound up become unbound and boundless.

How in the world could this be possible? In our own natural

strength and ability it is impossible. But there is another aspect: Our spirits have been made alive in Christ, and the Holy Spirit works His character within us.

"The Christian life is an ongoing walk of faith day by day," Jesus was saying.

> "Through the Holy Spirit you will bear supernatural fruit in this season when no one expects much. But if you say to this mountain be taken up and thrown into the sea and do not doubt in your heart but believe that what you say will come to pass, it will be done for you. Whatever you ask for in prayer you will receive."

Are you praying for healing? For direction? For saving faith in the heart of a loved one? Through fruit, which comes from fellowship with your Friend the Holy Spirit, you will have the character that builds faith to believe in answered prayer.

Jesus was the firstborn of a new generation of which we are members. By walking along with the Holy Spirit we are not counting on our own natural ability to do anything. We are trusting in the God of glory who is in us and with us. And so, we can go about expecting to do great things. Have faith, He said, and you will do great things.

Talk about a new beginning! That is the reality of the outpouring of the Spirit received in earthen vessels. Of course to receive these heavenly spiritual endowments, every person must first enter a personal relationship with the Giver and be filled with Him.

The Lord is calling us to experience Him as He really is. And with Him, there is not a single impossibility in existence. So what are you facing that seems impossible? Welcome the Holy Spirit to invade like a rushing river, overflowing the banks of the circumstances that have you hemmed in.

ENDURING FRUIT

It is good for us to take stock of the fruit in our lives. How about it? Are we handling that difficult insurance matter with patience? Are we extending kindness to the mom with three restless kids in the grocery store? Are we exhibiting peace when the economy makes finances tight?

True spiritual worship brings us into fellowship, and in fellowship we receive revelation. But every step of the way is an act of faith on our part. The lesson of the fig tree is that we can bear fruit in every season because God is with us.

As we grow, letting the Lord prune and shape us, we will know love all-encompassing, joy at all times, peace in the midst of every circumstance, patience when all other patience is failing, kindness when the whole world has turned to cruelty, goodness when moral confusion abounds, faithfulness when betrayal is on every side, gentleness in the face of harshness and self-control when discipline is no more.

Prayer

Lord, as I abide in You, may I bear true fruit of the Spirit of Christ. May the divine nature of God's Son be formed in my life as I yield to Your Spirit. May I have the grace to say no to my flesh. May the waters of the Holy Spirit bring forth love made evident in joy, peace, patience, gentleness, goodness, faithfulness and self-control. May I increase every day in being more and more like Christ, bringing Him glory.

Chapter 7

GIFTS AND MORE GIFTS

Have you ever made a comment like this? "Something told me to back up those new documents on my computer." Or: "I was going to take the main highway, but something told me to take the back route." As often as not, any time you followed one of these nudges, you were very glad later.

If you have sensed helpful impressions like these, you have heard the voice of your Friend, the Holy Spirit. What is more, the Bible describes this kind of impartation of information as just one of the many gifts that followers of Jesus can expect to have.

God gives supernatural treasures liberally to each of His children: gifts of the Spirit. These are like fabulous jewels purified by fire and loosed from the depths of the earth—and these treasures are yours. He is waiting to help you discover them.

One of the first times I, Mahesh, ministered at a particular church in London, the senior pastor introduced me, I walked to the podium and I began to speak.

Now, you should know that I grew up in East Africa, in Kenya, and I speak Swahili. Even so, I had not planned on speaking that Sunday morning in London in Swahili. From the puzzled expressions before me, I think the people who had gathered for worship were surprised as well!

I greeted them and started mentioning a few things—in particular that God was planning to use someone who was listening in a strategic way. I was not surprised at the Holy Spirit dropping thoughts into my head that He wanted me to share, but, still, part of me was saying, *What are you doing? Hello? This is London, England. You are not in East Africa.*

After a bit I reverted to English, but I was kind of hitting myself for such a peculiar start to my time there.

Following the service, the pastor introduced me to a man who said that he wanted to meet me. It was the attorney general of Kenya who was visiting London and happened to attend that church that morning. He told me that he felt very blessed that someone had greeted him in his own language. He said he could not wait to meet me and tell me that his heart had been touched by the words of encouragement that I had given.

That particular moment of following the Holy Spirit's nudge that morning was to speak to this man. He was already the attorney general of the whole nation of Kenya, but God was going to use him in more of a strategic way. When the Holy Spirit gave me the knowledge of certain information and encouraged me to share it, He was giving me a gift that I could use to bless someone else.

Now you might not get a nudge to minister to someone in Swahili, but you might have a word of direction for a friend at just the right time. Or you might have great faith that God will work through a difficult situation. These instances are gifts from the Holy Spirit so that we can help one another.

In this chapter we want to help you recognize the gifts that the Holy Spirit has given you and encourage you to be excited about using them. In the next chapter, we will look at specific steps to develop their use.

The Giver, the Gifts and the Glory

People who use the gifts that the Holy Spirit gives are sometimes referred to as being *anointed*, which means being set apart with special ability for the purposes of God. This anointing is available for everyone.

The Holy Spirit gives spiritual gifts in order to edify His people individually, and, in the larger context, to build His Church. The Church is a living organism, and the way to grow it successfully is not so much to organize as it is to recognize!

It begins with recognizing who we are in Christ, recognizing who He is in God, recognizing what He has done, recognizing our high calling, recognizing we have a place, a function and a fit, and recognizing He has given us each specific gifts.

We know this from the words of Paul:

> Now there are varieties of gifts, but the same Spirit. And there are varieties of ministries, and the same Lord. There are varieties of effects, but the same God who works all things in all persons.
>
> 1 Corinthians 12:4, NASB

The giver of gifts is God, the provider is Christ through His cross and resurrection, and the administrator is the Holy Spirit. Therefore, the gifts are holy. They carry the essence of God and His glory.

Not only does the Bible say that we have gifts, it tells us not to neglect them. In fact it says to "stir up" the gifts. The gifts are to be recognized, received and exercised. We begin to get a bit of a foretaste about eternal riches as we are filled with the Spirit, live lives that bear fruit and use the gifts.

The Bible describes three basic categories of supernatural gifts. As we mentioned, God decides who is best suited for which gifts and determines how our gifts correlate with the gifts He gives others so that we might complement and build up each other.

The three categories are the purpose gifts, the power gifts and the person gifts.

There are seven unique *purpose gifts*—every person has at least one. Discovering your primary purpose gift will help explain why you do what you do and help you see how you do it and how you can do it better.

As the gift-giver, the Holy Spirit presents nine various demonstrations of miraculous empowering. These are the *power gifts*. This means He gives supernatural ability to our minds and bodies. We access, in a moment, His higher knowledge, greater wisdom, good guidance, insight for the future and even physical healing that is beyond our personal capacity.

Jesus plants five kinds of persons—*person gifts*—as masterbuilders in the midst of His people. They work together with God to make His house into a glorious dwelling place.

The Bible refers to all God's gifts in terms of the word *grace*. Grace is an eternal characteristic of God Himself. He imparts Himself to us through gifts that enable us to live fuller lives.

Since grace is the fountain out of which the Holy Spirit gives us gifts, it makes sense that wherever the gifts of God are apparent, they evoke thanksgiving and worship and never self-promotion.

God Himself is a glorious community of interrelated persons—Father, Son and Spirit—yet He is One. Likewise, His gifts interrelate. The promotion of one to the exclusion of the others can lead to an unbalanced situation in a family, a business or a community. All are given to the Body and all are equally important.

Let's explore and identify these wonderful gifts that are ours to use. We will help you begin to find exactly that place of rest and peace and fruitfulness where you fit in.

THE PURPOSE GIFTS

The seven purpose gifts, listed in Romans 12:6–8, apply to all believers. They explain why we do things the way we do them.

> Since we have gifts that differ according to the grace given to us, each of us is to exercise them accordingly: if *prophecy,* according to the proportion of his faith; if *service,* in his serving; or he who *teaches,* in his teaching; or he who *exhorts,* in his exhortation; he who *gives,* with liberality; he who *leads,* with diligence; he who *shows mercy,* with cheerfulness.
>
> NASB, emphasis added

These gifts are prophecy, service, teaching, exhorting, giving, leading and mercy. Each one expresses a unique aspect of the nature of God. He puts them in us as uniquely designed personalities to express His nature, they offer insight into the primary way we view the world and they interact with it and with each other.

Nobody knows you better than you. God has designed you as a specialized package of destiny. He crafted your particular personality as a container for supernatural gifts. Discovering your purpose gifts is directly connected to recognizing what makes you thrive, feel alive and experience true fulfillment!

A wise man said, "If people can't see what God is doing, they stumble all over themselves. But when they attend to what He reveals, they are most blessed" (Proverbs 29:18, THE MESSAGE). Your most blessed state of living comes when you are doing what God has designed you to do. In that place, the gifts He has put in you will empower you to accomplish your purpose for living. Discovering your purpose gifts is a key to living your dreams.

As you read further in this section, you will probably recognize characteristics that ring true for you or describe someone you know well. We each have a unique blend of gifts that when fitted together like pieces of a puzzle with others' gifts will make visible the whole. The beauty of this is that it means none of us carries the burden alone, but we are interdependent with one another to fulfill God's ultimate purpose. The flip side of this is that none of us can truly find our purpose and mission as lone rangers. Nor can we operate if we are trying to fit in a place that does not match our unique "shape" or purpose gifting.

Recently a television commercial caught our eye as a humorous example of how purpose giftings relate to the building and operating of God's spiritual family. The storyline shows a man in counseling. He is lying on the couch sharing his deepest anxieties and hurts. His counselor is a former drill sergeant whose primary purpose gift is *not* mercy. His method of counseling is to yell, throw things and tell the man to grow up and get over it.

Obviously, this sketch is an extreme example, but the contrast of the drill sergeant with the expected persona of a personal counselor is a little like what happens when you expect someone whose purpose gift is prophecy to fill a role that would be better served by someone whose primary purpose gifting is exhortation or showing mercy.

Each one of us has a particular anointing from the Father in one or more of these areas so that we might minister to one another. The gifting is individual but it is for all. That is a theme that we find with the gifts again and again. They come to us individually but they are not for us individually.

These gifts are not the outcome of one's own natural instincts or personality. Once you have been born again, you begin to discover that there is a divine unction upon you that that has been given specifically by the Holy Spirit. You have been given, by God, an "unction to function" as He wills to bring forth His glory.

Having one particular gifting does not exclude you from participating in the others; it just lets you know that your natural inclination is to be attentive to and engage in the world around you through a particular grid.

In our local church body, for instance, we discovered that only 6 percent of the members of our congregation have the purpose gift of service. But perhaps because our church family emphasizes Jesus' model of servant leadership, everywhere you look, someone is involved in serving—and with great joy and enthusiasm.

God has created us as human beings to interrelate, to have communion with others and with Him. Not one of us in and of ourselves is meant to be full and complete; all of us fully and completely contribute something unique and valuable to the whole. That is the thing about the gifts of the Spirit.

Find Your Purpose Gift

Here is a simple way to assess your dominant areas of purpose gifting. These are characteristics of persons who have these gifts and some cautions for their use. You will likely identify with one or two of these descriptions. It also will help you understand the actions of some of the people around you.

Prophecy

The primary purpose gift of prophecy involves perceiving right and wrong and speaking truth. People with this gift are hardwired to recognize compromise or mixed motives. They have a high standard of excellence and feel obligated to call others to comply with their sense of right and wrong.

Characteristics

- Sees everything as either black or white with no gray areas
- Easily reads the motives or intentions behind others' actions
- Is outspoken and direct; does not mince words
- Has strong convictions and standards
- Regards the Bible as uncompromising standard for all truth, belief and action

Cautions

- Has exacting standards that are hard for others or themselves to reach
- Can be judgmental and blunt
- Tends to be unyielding to others' opinions

Service

The purpose gift of serving contributes to the functioning of the Body in practical ways. People with this gift are "others" focused and love to give their time and strength to meet the immediate needs of others. Servers are responsible, willing helpers who find joy in assisting, following instructions and fulfilling others' needs.

Characteristics

- Readily identifies practical needs and fills them
- Prefers not to be in charge of projects or in leadership
- Likes short-term, immediate goals
- Has high energy and stamina to stick with a project to completion
- Is usually a perfectionist and detail-oriented

Cautions

- Has a hard time saying no to requests for help
- Can neglect personal and family needs while helping others
- Can be easily hurt if he or she does not receive recognition and affirmation for service

Teaching

The person with the purpose gift of teaching analyzes, organizes and creates systems for information. This person is motivated to learn, research and share knowledge with others. People with this gifting approach problems from an abstract perspective and are sticklers for accuracy and validating facts. The teacher's ability to study and apply Scripture is vital to explain truth for understanding and application in the lives of others.

Characteristics

- Likes to analyze and organize information into a system
- Loves to study and research and has the natural ability to retain information
- Is concerned for accuracy and will validate questionable information or facts with personal research

- Has higher regard for biblical examples than for everyday life and is concerned when Scripture is used out of context
- Is gifted intellectually

Cautions

- Can be legalistic
- Can be intellectually proud and slow to accept others' viewpoints
- Tends to be idealistic and abstract and neglect the practical day-to-day application of truth to real life

Exhorting

The person with the purpose gift of exhorting, or encouraging, helps others realize their full potential and value in God. People with this gift instill vision in those they counsel and give a set course of action to get there. Their focus is on helping others mature and grow.

Characteristics

- Accepts and loves people unconditionally
- Has positive and optimistic outlook
- Likes practical "how-to" steps to solve problems
- Is a good communicator
- Encourages others to reach their full potential

Cautions

- Tends to become overbearing in enthusiasm to help others
- Can be outspoken and opinionated
- Can be overly self-confident

Giving

The purpose gift of giving expresses itself in a desire to mobilize material goods, finances and resources for the needs of God's work and people. The giver finds joy in meeting others' financial needs. The giver has a strong sense of quality and value and is an excellent manager of resources and investments.

Characteristics

- Generously gives time, money, assets, energy and love to help others
- Likes to give anonymously
- Is quick to identify and meet needs
- Values quality and investment
- Has natural and God-given wisdom for finances

Cautions

- May pressure others to give
- May want to control how gifts are used
- Can use financial contributions to avoid other responsibilities

Leading

The purpose gift of leading, or administration, is oriented toward achieving goals, coordinating resources and people, and organizing processes. People with this gifting enjoy leading and are excellent at delegating, making decisions, planning projects and helping others work together toward a common goal.

Characteristics

- Has big-picture mentality
- Focuses on long-term goals

- Does not enjoy the routine; likes new challenges
- Will assume leadership responsibility if none is apparent
- Is able to communicate, delegate and organize resources to accomplish a task

Cautions

- Can see people as objects to achieve goals
- Can become a workaholic
- Tends to be a type-A personality who will drive self and others

Mercy

The purpose gift of mercy extends compassion toward people in physical, spiritual or emotional distress. People with this gifting are sensitive to the emotional needs of others, and will go out of their way to protect people's feelings. They tend to be gentle and empathetic in dealing with people, and avoid conflict.

Characteristics

- Is concerned for others' emotional states or needs
- Avoids conflict or confrontation
- Is drawn to people who are hurting or distressed
- Always looks for good in others
- Tends to see life in shades of gray rather than black and white

Cautions

- Tends to be sensitive and easily hurt by others
- Can take up other people's hurts and offenses
- Tends to let feelings run ahead of facts
- May compromise values to avoid hurting others' feelings

Once you realize what you are designed for, you will have greater insight and direction concerning relationships, work and where and how you fit into the Body, your family, profession and calling. Understanding your purpose gifts makes your contribution more meaningful to you and to others.

THE POWER GIFTS

The nine power gifts are demonstrations of the fact that God is working with and through us. Some people may be particularly gifted in certain areas, but, as with the purpose gifts, anyone might be touched by God to use any of the gifts at any time.

The power gifts are listed in 1 Corinthians 12.

> The manifestation of the Spirit is given to each one for the profit of all: for to one is given *the word of wisdom* through the Spirit, to another *the word of knowledge* through the same Spirit, to another *faith* by the same Spirit, to another *gifts of healings* by the same Spirit, to another *the working of miracles*, to another *prophecy*, to another *discerning of spirits*, to another *different kinds of tongues*, to another *the interpretation of tongues*. But one and the same Spirit works all these things, distributing to each one individually as He wills.
>
> 1 Corinthians 12:4–11, emphasis added

Paul affirms that God is the giver. He gives. He takes the initiative to give gifts to every single person who calls on Him. What does He give? The manifestation of the Spirit. What does that mean? It means that God wants to be on display in you and through you. And He will demonstrate it by giving you spiritual gifts to exhibit, to enjoy, to use for His glory and for your good and blessing.

Why does He do this? It is not just for our benefit. It is "for the common good." The Lord longs for the whole of mankind to begin to taste and see His goodness, so He gives gifts that demonstrate His wonderful nature.

As *The Message* so wonderfully states:

> God's various gifts are handed out everywhere; but they all originate in God's Spirit. God's various ministries are carried out everywhere; but they all originate in God's Spirit. God's various expressions of power are in action everywhere; but God himself is behind it all. Each person is given something to do that shows who God is: Everyone gets in on it, everyone benefits. All kinds of things are handed out by the Spirit, and to all kinds of people! The variety is wonderful:
>
> wise counsel
> clear understanding
> simple trust
> healing the sick
> miraculous acts
> proclamation
> distinguishing between spirits
> tongues
> interpretation of tongues.
>
> All these gifts have a common origin, but are handed out one by one by the one Spirit of God. He decides who gets what, and when.
>
> 1 Corinthians 12:4–11, THE MESSAGE

The power gifts are unique, specific demonstrations of supernatural grace in a particular moment in time. You may be familiar with several of these, such as the impression or nudge to take a certain course of action. The biblical name for that is "word of knowledge." When you understand what to do with that word of knowledge, you have embraced a "word of wisdom" from the Holy Spirit.

Other manifestation gifts, such as "discerning of spirits," are no less mysterious when you understand the purpose of these gifts. Power gifts flow out of the presence of the Spirit of the Lord to do His work among us.

Three of the power gifts have to do with the mind, knowing:

- Word of wisdom
- Word of knowledge
- Discerning of spirits

Three of the power gifts have to do with the mouth, speaking:

- Prophecy or proclamation
- Tongues
- Interpretation of tongues

Three of the power gifts have to do with the hand, doing:

- Working of miracles
- Gifts of healing
- Faith

As with all of the gifts, no one is greater than the others.

RECOGNIZE THE POWER GIFTS

The power gifts are different from the purpose and person gifts in that they are brief, dramatic demonstrations of God's power at a particular moment. Here are some characteristics of the gifts and some cautions for their use.

The Word of Wisdom

The word of wisdom, or a gift of wise counsel, is a sudden understanding of the best way to proceed or communicate in a situation. It comes by the Spirit and exceeds natural understanding or personal experience. It is a little piece of God's whole wisdom.

You may suddenly have understanding of how to respond or act in a situation of which you have no natural knowledge or experience. You may find yourself counseling a friend or co-worker and hear yourself speaking with wisdom or counsel that you know is not your own. (It is at these moments that you wish you had a recorder going so you could remember what you said!)

During a ministry trip to Singapore, I, Mahesh, was invited to a dignitary's home. His family had asked me if I would come pray for him. Unbeknownst to me, the dignitary had passed away several days before!

To say I was surprised when I arrived and was ushered into the room where he lay would be a huge understatement. However, the Lord gave me wisdom in that situation. I prayed with the family, and as I left, I began walking backward out of the room. My mind was noting this as I was doing it: *I am walking backward out of the room.*

Well, that was the Holy Spirit's wisdom. In that culture, I later learned, it would have been very offensive and dishonoring to have turned my back on the dignitary's body. I did not have natural knowledge of that protocol, but I had the Holy Spirit guiding me with His wisdom.

Characteristics

- Gives a quick understanding of what to do in a situation
- Is useful for insight and counsel
- Helps the user to be considered trustworthy and dependable

Cautions

- People can be slow in the call to action
- Knowing the "how" to do something does not necessarily translate into knowing the "when." Can tend to get caught up in the details and delay moving forward in a timely manner

The Word of Knowledge

The gifts of the word of knowledge and the word of wisdom differ. Knowledge gives facts; wisdom directs. So you might say that the difference between the two is that the word of knowledge gives information, and the word of wisdom gives counsel about what to do with it.

This is a case where the gifts of the Spirit often blend together, and we may not be able to see exactly where one stops and another starts.

When the word of knowledge brings information or a fact to mind, it may come as an impression. You might, for instance, wake up and be thinking about a friend. Understanding that the Spirit often gives words of knowledge gently, dropping them into our minds like our own thoughts, you look at it more closely and realize you are concerned for her safety. You begin to pray for her.

Later that week you find out that your friend was in a fender bender that very morning and that your thoughts and prayers were directed by the Holy Spirit through the gift of a word of knowledge.

Sometimes the Holy Spirit's voice can be almost unmistakable. One father told us this story:

> The Bible says that the Lord will give His angels charge over us to keep us in all of our ways. I can attest to that truth as He has sent His angels to watch over our two elder children, Tasha and Antonio.

My wife and I were with our two younger children in Florida. Our two older children were at home. On Saturday morning, I was awakened by the Holy Spirit and in an instant I had a vision of my youngest child falling into an alligator pit. Suddenly I saw a huge hand reach down and grab her before she could hit the bottom of the pit and place her right back in the observation area.

The Holy Spirit said, *Start praying for your children. Bind accidents of all sorts.* So I did as the Holy Spirit commissioned me to do.

On Sunday afternoon my phone rang. It was my son, Antonio. I bolted upright when I heard him say, "Daddy, Tasha and I were just in a head-on collision."

Needless to say my heart nearly stopped. They said that they were both okay, but Antonio was banged up a bit. We packed our bags and hurried home.

That night the kids gave us the details. While coming home from church, their car had hydroplaned and veered off into oncoming traffic, and that is when the impact took place. The doors were jammed, and both children were trapped inside the car as it began filling with smoke.

Other motorists actually looked on without trying to help. So my kids began to call on Jesus. The doors that were jammed suddenly opened and Antonio and Tasha walked away with nominal injuries.

Jesus saved our children from death. He woke me up the morning before to pray for and to cover them. "Behold I am with you always even unto the end of the age." Surely the Lord was with our children on that Sunday. We are so excited about Jesus and what the future holds for all of us and our children.

This testimony, by the way, is indicative of the progression of using the Holy Spirit's gifts. The word of knowledge produced conviction and preparation in the one who heard it. Dramatic results followed. Then it brought rejoicing and glory to God.

Characteristics

- Gives clear facts
- Reveals knowledge about a person or situation, past or present

Caution

- People might act on what they think the information means, rather than wait for understanding of how best to proceed

Discerning of Spirits

Have you ever been in a situation where you felt your hair stood on end for no apparent reason? Or have you had an interaction with a person that seemed normal on the surface, but left you feeling creepy inside?

Or, on the positive side, have you heard someone say something, and your heart skipped a beat with joy, excitement or expectation?

These are examples of how the gift of discernment works. You suddenly know the spiritual dynamics behind the scenes. This may be a general feeling on a gut level, or very specific knowledge either in a vision or impression. This can be for reassurance, protection or to help you know how to pray in a situation.

Five types of spirits we can clearly discern are the Holy Spirit, the human spirit, holy angels, fallen angels and demons. A biblical example of discernment of a human spirit is when Jesus discerned that Nathaniel's spirit was pure, without guile.

More than any other spirit, we do well to discern when the Holy Spirit is present, speaking and acting. John the Baptist saw the Spirit descend to rest on Jesus the day He was baptized. Like John, we want to recognize when He is at work. Sometimes He does things unexpectedly and unusually. When that happens, people who cannot discern it might dismiss what happened or miss what God is giving in the moment.

If we have the gift of discerning of spirits we can know when it is God and His angels, or the human spirit, or evil spirits at work. Then we can respond in the right way.

Characteristics

- Reveals the real voice behind the words; answers the question: Is this something that is spiritually good or evil?

- Perceives motives and spiritual influences operating in a situation

Caution

- Persons with this gift can start to think that everything has a negative spiritual motive or influence behind it

Prophecy

The power gift of prophecy is given to declare what God is saying in the moment. It is usually connected to particular persons and events and often concerns the future. God says it, then you say it. God shows it, and you see it and tell it. Every prophecy is only part of the picture, and every prophetic word is subject to judgment from Scripture and seasoned Christians' interpretation.

This gift may come to you as an impression or a "hunch" about a person or situation. It may come as a dream that either gives you insight into the past or gives you instruction for the present. Or you may find yourself living out your dream in a matter of days or weeks only to realize the Lord prepared you ahead of time.

Frequently the gift of prophecy will be activated as you read Scripture. A particular verse will suddenly come alive and speak to your heart with a particular message of hope, encouragement or promise. Often, you will find that the word the Holy Spirit spoke to you is also a word of encouragement for someone you meet later that day or week.

This gift is for all believers, so as you learn to recognize and hear the Holy Spirit's voice in your own life, expect to flow more and more in this gift.

As with other manifestations of the gifts be aware that there is true prophecy and false prophecy. One comes from God and the other from either the counterfeiter or just human wisdom. To distinguish between them you need discerning of spirits together with basic knowledge of Scripture.

Characteristics

- Gives instant revelation in words and pictures that reveal spiritual realities
- May contradict the natural senses
- Always brings strength, courage and comfort to the hearers

Caution

- Prophecy can be misinterpreted by the one who receives it, or by those who hear it

Tongues

The power gift of tongues allows the Holy Spirit to bypass the human mind and speak through us in a supernatural language to say what is on God's mind. There are many kinds of languages from the Holy Spirit, just as there are different human languages. For the power gift of tongues to be effective communication when used publicly, it must be interpreted.

Tongues are also a gift for use in personal prayer times—a

devotional or supernatural language that draws the user closer to God. In this way the Holy Spirit can help us by filling our hearts and minds with words not of our own design. Romans 8:26–27 outlines this blessing:

> The Spirit also helps us in our weaknesses. For we do not know what we should pray for as we ought, but the Spirit Himself makes intercession for us with groanings which cannot be uttered. Now He who searches the hearts knows what the mind of the Spirit is, because He makes intercession for the saints according to the will of God.

This gift is particularly helpful when we have no idea how to pray or we cannot express the depth of our hearts in our natural language. Praying in our supernatural prayer language is different from the power gift of tongues, and it does not require interpretation. We recommend that everyone spend some time praying in tongues every day. It is easy to do and a great way to fellowship with your Friend, the Holy Spirit, during commutes, exercise or worship.

Characteristics

- Comes suddenly as spoken words demonstrated in public worship
- Is followed in public by the power gift of interpretation so that everyone in the gathering can hear it and receive benefit

Caution

- The apostle Paul warned believers to be considerate of proper protocol in public so their use of this gift would be helpful and not disruptive

Interpretation of Tongues

This gift is the essential counterpart of the power gift of tongues. The person given the gift of interpretation works like a translator, allowing the hearers to understand what the Holy Spirit is saying. Different functions of the interpretation of tongues would include intercession, praise, exhortation and rebuke.

Characteristic

- Gives human understanding of the gift of tongues

Caution

- A person could make up the interpretation or add his or her own human insight or opinion to the interpretation

Working of Miracles

Working of miracles and the next gift, gifts of healings, both plural terms, indicate that there are multiple gifts of different miracles and multiple gifts of various kinds of healing. There are plenty to go around; everybody can participate and be used by God.

The power gift of working of miracles is a supernatural act given by the Holy Spirit through the hands of a human that changes the natural order. Miracles operate in conjunction with faith, and the gift of miracles is often accompanied by the gift of faith.

Miracles replace physical things either in the body or in other physical realms, such as when the bread and fish were multiplied by Jesus to feed large crowds on two occasions. The Holy Spirit makes something out of nothing.

How many times have you been in a situation and thought, *I need a miracle!*? We have probably all had that thought—for some of us, many times in our lives. Basically what we are saying in that moment is, "I need something to happen *now* that will get me out of this mess!" And, actually, that is what a miracle is—an immediate, supernatural intervention of the Holy Spirit that gets us or someone else out of the "messes" that happen in this world.

Miracles are often centered on healing, such as when blind eyes are instantly healed, deaf ears are opened or tumors disappear while you watch. But miracles can also be for other "messes." In fact, Jesus' first miracle turned six jars of water into wine. That might not seem like a high priority to us when we are praying for a loved one suffering from cancer, but for that bridegroom who would have faced humiliation and shame for running out of wine at his wedding, it was the miracle he needed.

We have experienced many miracles in our lives, especially in the dramatic intervention of God in the lives of our children, but one of the most amazing miracles we have seen in more than thirty years of ministry occurred when I, Mahesh, was ministering in Pakistan.

We were in one of the most impoverished areas I have ever been in my life. Everywhere I looked I saw desperate spiritual and physical need. One woman in particular stood out to me. She was a beggar who sat along the road I travelled every day.

One day I stopped to take a picture of her. She was blind; she had been born without eyeballs. She was a symbol to me of the deep need and darkness that covered the people of that area.

The last day of my outreach there the Holy Spirit led me at the beginning of my meeting to pray for the region to be set free from darkness. As soon as I finished praying, I saw a lone figure come forward out of the vast crowd. I knew the prayer I had just prayed had been prompted by the Holy Spirit, but the proof came as the woman I had photographed on the side of the road walked forward seeing! Where her sockets had been empty, she now had deep, dark, lovely eyes and could see perfectly. That was a miracle!

Characteristics

- Is a dramatic, instant, physical demonstration of God's direct, supernatural power
- Brings something into being out of nothing

Caution

- People sometimes attribute to God unusual acts that are really of human initiation. The Bible warns that the counterfeiter, Satan, sometimes pulls magic stunts to try to draw people away from Jesus. Real miracles always draw people to Jesus only.

Gifts of Healings

Healing means a change in a physical body. A person is sick, infirmed or something is broken or diseased: The gift of healing restores that one to perfect health.

There are various types of gifts for various types of healings. One person, for instance, may have a gift of healing eyes. In that case the person might pray for every kind of eye infirmity and see those eyes healed. Other gifts of healings may address categories of diseases like cancer, broken bones, digestive issues, mental illness. Or, a person may have a general gift that brings physical healing of any kind.

Gifts of healings differ from workings of miracles in that the healing is often a gradual process rather than an instantaneous change.

We have, for instance, seen many people healed of various eye diseases such as glaucoma or macular degenerative disease. These medical conditions are typically progressive and are not reversible, so when people come back seeing, we know the Lord has touched them with His power for healing. This kind of healing is different from a miracle, such as the Pakistani woman who instantly had eyes where there had been nothing before.

Characteristics

- Fixes whatever is sick, broken or diseased in a person's body
- Produces physical relief and great joy
- Makes God's personal presence and power real

Caution

- Some may discount the value of medical intervention. We always advise people to seek healing through prayer and medical treatment when needed, especially with children, critical illnesses or accidents.

Faith

There are three kinds of faith in Scripture. First, God gives everyone a measure of faith from the moment we first come to Him, and we can always get more faith as we read His Word (see Romans 10:17). Next there is faith that develops as a fruit of your relationship with the Holy Spirit (see Galatians 5:22). And then there is the power gift of faith listed in 1 Corinthians 12:9.

The power gift of faith is distinguished from the other types of faith in that it is a special infusion of faith for a particular moment or action. You could compare it to the rush of excitement you experience when you first fall in love or hear particularly good news. In that moment you feel as though you can do anything.

In the spiritual dimension, the power gift of faith is like that. The Holy Spirit will fill you with a certainty that all is well—you know that you can pray and expect to receive what you have asked for. It does not matter how dire the circumstances or impossible the odds. You know that what God has spoken will come to pass.

The gift of faith moves aside all obstacles and problems. It changes natural circumstances into supernatural breakthrough in one instant. This kind of faith is actually God's own faith in action through a human vessel.

A seed of God's faith dropped into your heart can move a mountain or bring a dead person back to life as it is God Himself exhibiting His faith in you. It is not the quantity, it is the quality. This gift usually operates through a spoken word and has creative power. It is a brief impartation for the purpose God wants to accomplish on the spot.

Characteristics

- Assures for certain that the impossible is easily accomplished *now*
- Is positive, forceful
- Produces immediate results

Caution

- Human presumption, which is the opposite of God's faith, can slip in

LEARNING TO FLOW IN THE POWER GIFTS

Shortly after I, Mahesh, was filled with the Holy Spirit, the Lord called me to work at the Lubbock State School for Children in Lubbock, Texas.

The children who lived there were tragic cases. Many were the children of heroin addicts. All of them were severely disabled and most were wards of the state, abandoned by their families.

When the Lord called me, I "heard" Him impress these words on my heart: *I am a Father to the fatherless. I am commissioning you as an ambassador of love to these little ones that the world has forgotten.* I soon found that as I made myself available to demonstrate God's love to these children, the Lord demonstrated His Fatherly care and love for them in a very practical way through the gifts of the Spirit. In the process, He set some of the children free from debilitating conditions, and I learned how to hear and flow in the leading of the Holy Spirit.

I remember one day in particular. I had just left the girls' dorm and walked over to the boys' dorm where I was in charge of setting up a behavior modification program. As I walked into the dorm, I heard an inner voice, like an impression, say, *Go back to Rose.*

Rose was the name of the girls' dorm I had just left. I did not realize that this was the voice of the Holy Spirit. I thought it was just a random thought and continued on with my business. Then a few minutes later I heard it again: *Go back to Rose.*

This time I thought it might be the Lord, so I said, "Lord, I just came from Rose. I have to finish this assignment."

Then I heard it a third time: *Go back to Rose—now!*

I was suddenly aware of the urgency of the Lord's voice. I quickly let my co-workers know where I was going and ran back to Rose. The scene that greeted me was frightening.

Many of the children in the home had the mental age of toddlers, but the physical size and strength of an adult. When a twenty-year-old child would throw a two-year-old tantrum, the child would be placed in a special room where he or she could be isolated for a bit in order not to endanger the other kids.

On this day, a volunteer foster grandparent had been visiting Penny, a darling, gentle little girl. At the end of their visit, the foster grandparent accidentally dropped Penny off at the wrong room. Instead of her dorm, she ushered this little girl into an isolation room where a violent older girl had just been placed. As the door locked behind her, Penny was face-to-face with a crazed girl who immediately began to beat her. Penny was deaf and mute and had no way to escape or call for help.

The Lord knew about this situation and had been speaking to me, giving me a word of knowledge to return to Rose before it was too late for Penny. When I did arrive, Penny had been savagely beaten. Her face was swollen and purple where the other girl had beaten her with her shoe. She wept in silent terror and agony.

We called for a doctor because she was in need of immediate care, but she would not let any of them touch her or come near except for me. I sat down next to her and said, "Penny, Jesus loves you." The moment I spoke those words, total peace filled the room. I also felt a sensation in my right hand, sort of like pins and needles, and I sensed energy was flowing out of my hand as I held Penny's hand.

Within a matter of moments, the appearance of her face began to change. The swelling began to disappear. The purple welts and bruises started changing from black and purple to dark red, to a perfectly normal skin tone. Every mark and bruise disappeared and she was completely healed right before our eyes!

There was no way that I could have known that that little girl's life was in danger. But her heavenly Father knew! The Holy Spirit gave me a word of knowledge that allowed me to intervene for Penny's life. Then He released His healing, miracle power to immediately touch and restore Penny's body.

The Holy Spirit wants to be with you and speak to you for the needs of those around you. He may be invisible, but He wants to make His presence known and show His love and care to others. He has chosen to do it through you! How? You demonstrate it through the power gifts.

The Person Gifts

This category of gifts is slightly different from the other two because Christ gives these gifts to His Church in the form of persons. The gifts are actually people in certain offices who help believers go about their various tasks for God's Kingdom. They help set the Church in order so that it is functioning and showing forth the glory of God in the earth.

In other words, exercising a particular gift such as prophecy or teaching is different from being a prophet or being a teacher.

Five types of persons are set apart by Christ and anointed by Him to help build, guide and strengthen our lives so we can flourish in God.

The person gifts are listed in the book of Ephesians:

> And He Himself gave some to be *apostles*, some *prophets*, some *evangelists*, and some *pastors* and *teachers*, for the equipping of the saints for the work of ministry, for the edifying of the body of Christ, till we all come to the unity of the faith and of the knowledge of the Son of God.
>
> Ephesians 4:11–13, emphasis added

The anointing or the oil of the Holy Spirit is on these persons to demonstrate Jesus, who is the ultimate, the consummate apostle, prophet, evangelist, pastor and teacher. Notice the purpose of these persons who are gifts: It is to make all of us successful as children of God. The fruit of these particular persons in our lives is to produce faith and intimate personal knowledge of Jesus as the Son of God.

These individuals are never self-appointed; they are appointed by God, anointed for their work and set in place by Him. You may know a gifted teacher who has touched your life. Or perhaps an evangelist came to your town, and you were gripped by his or her words. As you grow in knowledge of the Holy Spirit, you will be able to recognize and receive into your life the ministry of the five-fold offices.

If God has called you to one of the people gifts, He will make it very clear. If you are an evangelist, you might find that people are eager to hear you talk about the Lord and implore you to come talk with them. If you are a pastor, perhaps your heart will burn with that desire.

The story is told of a shoemaker who came to salvation under the ministry of Martin Luther. He asked Luther if he should leave his talent for shoemaking behind and become a monk.

Luther advised against such an idea. He said something along the lines of: "No, God has blessed you as a shoemaker. Be the best shoemaker. Be honest and treat people with dignity. Glorify God in the work He has called you to do."

In other words, you might enjoy pursuing any of these gifts as one of the many aspects of service, but if God has called you to be a plumber or a photographer, a homemaker or a hotel manager, bring God honor through that work.

Here is an overview of these five person gifts.

Apostle

Apostles are God's big builders. They have a big-picture approach to what God is up to. Apostles are assigned to specific tasks and sometimes to particular people groups as their life's work. Local church congregations are the greatest jewels in an apostle's eye. Their tasks always focus on building Jesus' Church and accomplishing His vision. Apostles are not tyrants or loners. Miracles follow them wherever they go.

Characteristics

- Has a "big-picture" vision
- Has long-term endurance
- Is blessed to perform unusual miracles as demonstrations of God's power
- Never undertakes self-promotion at the expense of God's gift or God's people

Cautions

- Can be reluctant to make sudden changes
- Can be overprotective of church resources
- Tends to be too quick to put one's own life on the line

Prophet

While the Bible encourages every believer to prophesy, a prophet is given the gift of regularly seeing and hearing what God is doing now or in the future.

This is not the same as being a "visionary." Prophets never lead. They come as servants to pastors and work in tandem with the vision and direction of apostles in the interest of lifting up Jesus. His or her revelation is a piece of the puzzle, not the whole picture. The revelation and spirit of real prophets is always a testimony to Jesus Himself (see Revelation 19:10).

Characteristics

- Sees pictures, dreams, visions
- Is uncompromising in truth
- Has revelation that gives strength, courage and comfort

Cautions

- Can have an overpowering personality

- Can mistakenly assume spiritual authority over a situation
- Tends toward acting on his or her own

Evangelist

The evangelist is God's harvesting machine. Getting people saved is the evangelist's food and drink. Evangelists are always introducing people to Jesus personally. They are key in changing lives and increasing the number of members of God's family.

Characteristics

- Is constantly sharing the message of Jesus with non-Christians
- Is often anointed with prophetic words, words of knowledge or gifts of healings and miracles to testify to the message of the Gospel

Cautions

- May expect everyone else to be involved only in missions or preaching the Gospel
- Can tend to operate as a lone ranger

Pastor

Pastors are God's sheep-keepers. Their job is to know, love, cover, correct and heal the members of God's flock. They supply nourishing and refreshing spiritual food and drink. They provide oversight and care toward weak or sickly members. They watch for spiritual predators or other dangers to the health of their flocks. They bring correction and discipline when and where it is necessary for church health.

Characteristics

- Shows loving devotion and integrity toward local church congregations of believers
- Has concern for the personal and corporate growth, blessing and prosperity of the ones being cared for

Cautions

- May be reluctant to delegate responsibility with authority to other members of the flock
- Can take on personally the whole weight of every member's burdens

Teacher

Teachers lay the foundation of spiritual knowledge by instructing us from the Bible. They help us understand the truth of the Bible and how to make it real in our lives.

Characteristics

- Loves to read, study, analyze and research Scripture
- Understands the Bible as the final authority of all God says and does
- Bases their personal faith and action on what the Bible presents

Cautions

- Can see their teaching as of greater value than the people being taught
- Can become fact-oriented and impersonal

A Picture of the Gift Giver

When we think about the Spirit giving gifts to everyone for the benefit of all, we cannot help but think of Bonnie's Aunt Hattie.

Aunt Hattie never missed any child's birthday, and there were a lot of nieces and nephews in the Elkins family. Aunt Hattie would drive to the child's home on his or her birthday with a special present, even if there was no party and even if no one else remembered. Aunt Hattie would show up with a gift she had chosen based on her personal knowledge and love of that child.

Every Christmas Aunt Hattie's nine siblings, their spouses and their children all gathered for family dinner. For months prior to that day, Aunt Hattie, from her own means, was shopping. And under the tree when it came to Santa time, there would be a special gift for each child with his or her name on it given in celebration of Christmas.

That is a good picture of the Holy Spirit as the distributor of God's gifts to us. His joy in this giving is boundless, and His knowledge of what to give when is incomparable.

This is your Friend, the Holy Spirit. As you learn to hear His voice more clearly, and begin to do as He directs you—sharing a story from the Bible that pops into your mind, warning a friend that a chosen path is not wise, praying for a sick colleague—you will soon see patterns in the way He leads you. Let your confidence build in hearing His voice and using the gifts that He leads you to use.

Now that we have better understanding of the gifts the Holy Spirit has given us, let's learn more about how to use them.

Prayer

Heavenly Father, thank You for creating me for Your unique purposes. Thank You for giving me spiritual gifts by Your Spirit to help me fulfill my God-given destiny. May I learn to recognize the gifts You have given so that I can find my place and function in the Church You are building. I pray for humility and love to grow in me so that I am always yielded to Your leading and always demonstrating Jesus through Your precious anointing in my life.

Chapter 8

OPEN THE PACKAGE

The Bible exhorts us to be hungry for the gifts, and to use them (see 1 Corinthians 12:31). We can exercise the gifts by discerning when, where and how the Spirit is leading. Jesus, as in all things, is our example. He used the gifts of the Holy Spirit perfectly.

Obviously He demonstrated the people gifts, the offices of apostle, prophet, evangelist, pastor, teacher. We see Him in His prophetic unction, for instance, when He is speaking of the end times and what is coming for Jerusalem. In His pastoral role we see Him as the great Shepherd of the sheep.

In purpose gifting, we see Him in His mercy ministry, showing compassion to all those who came to Him for healing and deliverance. He is the Ultimate Servant: We see Him giving His life on the cross. We see Jesus teaching His disciples, breaking things down for them, explaining the Kingdom of God to them.

We see Him using all of the power gifts. He discerned what was in the hearts of men. He cast out demons. He healed the blind and lame.

Now, as His Body on earth, believers all share in the gifts so that the fullness of God will be evident to the world. Each different part of His Body has different gifts; all are needed for the Lord's work to be complete.

No spiritual gift is of lesser or greater value than another. Receiving any gift from the Holy Spirit is a high privilege. These grace gifts are appropriated by faith and administrated by the resident Lord of the Church (see 1 Corinthians 12:11, 18).

It boils down to this: We have been given gifts, we have been given grace by God according to those gifts, and with that we have been given a measure of faith. All that is left is for us is to exercise the grace that God has given us, exercise the measure of faith that He has given us and use the gifts He has given us.

Remember: Once the gifts are given, they are not taken back, so even if you were once sure of your gifting and then found yourself in a long, hot, dry season and all of that zip sort of faded into the background, the gift has not been retracted. His gifts are divinely appointed, divinely ordained.

Now, here are steps to help you develop your gifting.

EIGHT STEPS TO USING THE GIFTS

We find that there are eight important steps that will help you begin to recognize and use the gifts the Spirit has given you.

Step One

The first one is to be filled and refilled with the Spirit of God. As we learn from Jesus' parable of the ten virgins, five of whom ran out of oil, we need to be filled continually with the Holy Spirit. Our infilling is not a one-time event, but an activity that we cultivate day to day as we commune with the Holy Spirit through prayer, Scripture reading, worship and being attentive to His voice.

Once you are filled and lit, like an oil lamp, your light needs to shine. Jesus said that no one would light a lamp and put it under a basket; you put it on a lampstand for everybody to see. Stay ready for God to use you in His service.

Step Two

The second step is a point of order. Rather than think about the gifts you have, think about what function God has appointed for you in His Body. In other words, you need to find the place where you fit.

There are many members in the Body, but different functions, and each of us must function according to the grace and faith given us (see Romans 12:3). Not everyone will be a "hand" in the Body, because then it would not have a "foot" or an "ear" (see 1 Corinthians 12:17).

When you are in the proper place, you will have great ease in using your gifts. Conversely, if you find that you often struggle for faith, or are in continual conflict with the people around you, perhaps you are not recognizing your place and the gifting God has given you. Are you trying to fill a place that God has not specially called you to?

Begin to recognize what your gifts are—your function, the place you fit. When you read the list of purpose gifts in the previous chapter, did one or two "feel right"? Did something resonate within you when you read certain descriptions?

What gives you great joy? Teaching? Helping someone get organized? Serving coffee to guests? Perceiving right or wrong in a situation? Having a word of encouragement for someone?

The gifts are a natural expression of who you are. When you find your right function, you will find that God has given you the gifting and proportional measure of faith that is necessary to do that particular function.

Step Three

Exercise the gifts He has given you to the fullest.

Know that God gives you gifts according to what He knows you can do with them. Jesus' parable shows us this in Matthew 25:15: "And to one [the master] gave five talents, to another two, and to another one, to each according to his own ability."

In other words, if you can use five talents the Holy Spirit will give you five; if you can use two, He will give you two. If you can use only one, He will give you one. But if you feel as though you are "only" a one-talent Christian right now, take heart. As you use your gifts, whether one or many, at 100 percent of your ability, they grow!

The Holy Spirit knows your circumstances. He knows your personality. He knows the purposes and dreams He has for you. He knows what you are capable of, and He does not ask more from you than He knows you can deliver. As you are faithful in what He has given, you will begin to receive more.

Perhaps when you read the power gift descriptions you thought, *I've experienced that before!* You might not have even known that the Holy Spirit was there helping you in that moment, but now you do. Get ready and be expectant of more. And when you do sense the Holy Spirit is anointing you to pray for healing or give a prophetic word to a friend, or you suddenly have discernment or knowledge for a situation, step out in faith that your Friend is right there with you to demonstrate the Father's heart and care through you in that moment.

Here is one example of a family that was led on a journey of healing as they followed the Holy Spirit in a time of physical need for their daughter:

> Katie, our fifteen-year-old daughter, plays high school basketball and volleyball. One morning she woke up with a painful, swollen foot. She had had no injury to cause it.

After numerous doctor visits and tests over a period of several months, Katie's doctor determined she had a compressed nerve in her ankle. Four different doctors tried a series of different treatments, but her condition grew worse.

This nerve compression became disabling for Katie. She needed crutches most of the time or a wheelchair for extended walking distances, and she needed pain medications around the clock. Five months after the onset of this pain, Katie's doctor performed a surgical procedure to try to decompress the nerve. The surgery caused that nerve to become so hypersensitive that she could not touch her foot without pain.

Throughout this ordeal, our family had nightly prayer meetings in Katie's bedroom. We prayed, believing for healing, spoke healing to Katie, thanked God for His mercy and praised Him every night.

Isaiah 40:31 was the Scripture we felt led to "stand on" in faith: "They that wait upon the Lord, shall renew their strength. They shall mount up with wings as eagles. They shall run and not be weary. They shall walk and not faint."

We attended a particular church service during this time and received prayer from our pastor. He told her she would get better over the next week, and that the Scripture for her to focus on was Isaiah 40:31.

We rejoiced when we heard "our" Scripture! What a confirmation! Within one week after the conference, Katie began walking. The sensitivity in her foot became normal, the pain subsided, and she began to gain strength in that leg.

We went back to her doctor, and he prescribed four weeks of physical therapy. She was recovering so fast that within a few weeks her doctor dismissed her from therapy and released her to participate fully in sports again.

She is walking, running, jumping, playing basketball, playing volleyball and making the mighty works of the Lord known to all our friends! We are praising and rejoicing in God's loving, healing power.

The Holy Spirit led Katie's family each step of the way, and the adventure became her healing testimony. Their Friend was there, directing their prayers with His Word, filling them with faith for her healing and confirming it all with their pastor's word of knowledge. All brought forth God's perfect pleasure: healing!

I, Mahesh, have often come across people in and out of the Church who do not believe in the gifts of the Spirit. I used to get a little upset when people would challenge me and say, "God doesn't heal today." Or, "The ability to prophesy no longer exists."

But now I just say, "Lord, if they don't want their talents, give them to me! If they don't want You, Holy Spirit, I will take more."

Step Four

Remember: The distribution of the gifts is done according to God's will.

First Corinthians 12:11 says that the Holy Spirit has distributed to each one individually as He wills. In Hebrews 2:4 we read that each function is intrinsically given by God, "bearing witness both with signs and wonders, with various miracles, and gifts of the Holy Spirit, according to His own will." Therefore, an essential part of using the gifts is to learn to be led continually by the Holy Spirit (see Romans 8:14).

Learning to recognize how the Holy Spirit is working in your life and the lives of others around you will allow you to rest in the purpose God has for you without getting locked into a rigid mold of what your gifting is and how you should function.

The good news is, you never have to worry about finding your place. Your gift will make room for you (see Proverbs 18:16). The Holy Spirit is the resident administrator of the Church, and He will equip you and lead you to contribute effectively as you yield to Him.

I, Bonnie, for example, have a primary purpose gift of serving. My primary power gift is prophecy, and my person gift is teacher. These three distinct giftings blend together like the colors of the rainbow. They do not prohibit me from serving or being helpful or Christlike in every situation. As I follow the voice of the Gift-Giver, they can serve to make me useful and functional for edification of the whole as I fit in my proper place and let them flow in liberty and love.

Step Five

Receive the gifts that are for everyone.

The apostle Paul teaches the Church that everybody should be prophesying, everybody should be speaking in tongues, and anyone who speaks in tongues publically should interpret. He says that he is teaching them the commandments of the Lord (see 1 Corinthians 14:37). That means that these gifts are God's will for all believers and just as relevant for you today as they were then.

A few years ago we were ministering in England. Our daughter Serah was with us and was part of a team of people who were praying for a dear friend who suffers from multiple sclerosis. They gathered around him and spent several minutes praying as the Holy Spirit led them.

After they finished, our friend said to the group, "You don't know this because you don't speak Arabic, but Serah was praying in perfect Arabic, 'Healing, Lord Jesus! Healing, Lord Jesus!'"

Serah was just as surprised as everyone else. She had been praying in her supernatural prayer language and had no idea that she was praying in Arabic. But this is an example of how the Holy Spirit used her to speak a message of hope and encouragement that our friend would hear and understand was directly from Him.

Step Six

Get moving in the anointing.

Paul instructs us to desire spiritual gifts, especially prophecy (see 1 Corinthians 14:1). If you seek a gift, simply ask and receive. Jesus assured us that the Father gives good gifts to His children who ask.

> "So I say to you, ask, and it will be given to you; seek, and you will find; knock, and it will be opened to you. For everyone who asks receives, and he who seeks finds, and to him who knocks it will be opened. If a son asks for bread from any father among you, will he give him a stone? Or if he asks for a fish, will he give him a serpent instead of a fish? Or if he asks for an egg, will he offer him a scorpion? If you then, being evil, know how to give good gifts to your children, how much more will your heavenly Father give the Holy Spirit to those who ask Him!"
>
> Luke 11:9–13

God is a good God. He gives good things to those who ask Him. God will never give you something evil when you ask for something good. Ask with confidence and faith. Be assured it is God's will for you to receive gifts of the Holy Spirit.

Step Seven

Exercise the gifts He gives.

Practice makes perfect. As you pray, believe you are receiving His gifts and then begin to use them.

Have you had some evidence in your lifetime that God has given you some spiritual gifts? Well, stir them up, because guess what? He has a lot more for you! You will blossom like an almond tree. Suddenly you will think, *God, I didn't know I could do that. I didn't know You would do that through me.*

One of our good friends, Amber, told us about the first time she had gotten a prophetic impression from the Lord. She had been at one of our services where we were teaching on hearing from the Lord. I, Bonnie, had just prayed for the congregation and asked them to pray to receive a prophetic word for the person sitting next to them.

Amber was terrified and decided that it was a good time to visit the restroom! She did not think that she could hear from the Lord.

After the service, Amber and her mother went to a café. Instead of a nice relaxing lunch, she and her mother were soon in a heated "discussion." As Amber's emotions rose, she prayed silently, *Lord, please help us!*

All of a sudden, Amber saw a quick vision in her mind's eye. It was of a bunch of helium balloons being popped with a pin. She had never had anything like that happen before, but she realized it was from the Lord.

She said, "Mom, I just got a picture. We're popping each other's balloons." That picture from the Lord turned the situation around. Neither of them had ever realized how their words were perceived by the other. Soon both were crying—and their relationship was restored.

Amber was overwhelmed. She had not asked God for a prophetic word, she had just asked for help. Now she knew she could hear God and had the evidence of how effectively His gift can work in bringing His healing, presence and peace to a situation.

There are needy people all around. The Lord will give you a word of encouragement or insight into how to pray for healing for their bodies.

As you begin to experience the leading of the Holy Spirit, we encourage to you keep a journal or diary to record the ways the Lord begins to speak to you and use you. Always be thankful, and rejoice in every miracle, word and encounter He gives you. The more you honor and acknowledge the Father and His gifts, the more He will release them in your life.

Step Eight

And lastly, love, love, love.

There is one reason for getting to know the Holy Spirit and moving in His power; there is one reason for being desirous of gifts and more gifts; there is one reason for the manifest anointing of glory and power on the Church: love, love, love.

Jesus said, "This is the way the world is going to know that you know Me, by your love for one another" (see John 13:35). Not by your great power, not by your great miracles. Those things are demonstrations that His Kingdom has come, but the motive and the end result for moving in the power of the Spirit is simply love for God and love for one another.

Love is always the motive for using the gifts—love toward God and love toward our fellow man. There should never be a conflict between love and spiritual gifts. First Corinthians 14:1 tells us to "pursue love, and desire spiritual gifts." The gifts of the Holy Spirit are channels through which love should flow.

USER CAUTION

When you take vitamins, the label will often direct you how to use them properly to enhance your health and strengthen your well-being. Too many, too much in the wrong way can actually counteract what they are intended for.

In a way the gifts of the Spirit, because they are spiritual and from God and huge in power, can be like that too. And so, the gift Manufacturer and Giver also sends them with a user-caution label.

Spiritual gifts are never given to glorify the one who uses them. The gifts bring glory to God alone and are also a means of edifying, or building up, His people. They are tools, not toys. They are gifts, not guarantees of anything. The gifts are never evidence of someone's character. They are divine graces that make manifest the glory and power of God.

While the gifts are expressions of God's power, once He gives them the recipient is the wielder. That means even the gifts of the Spirit can be mishandled if the one who receives them is intent only on personal desires.

Faith and grace are given to the believer in measures equal to the gifts the Holy Spirit administers. Conversely, if someone tries to operate outside of the area of his or her spiritual gifting, it is likely that the same measure of grace and faith will not be present.

God is giving fresh grace to help us understand why we are hungry for demonstrations of His power. It is not because we want to be seen as something great, not because we are expecting the Holy Spirit to come and affirm how wonderful we are.

All of that is unnecessary. He is increasing His glory and refueling His hungry and thirsty seekers with His divine presence and power so that we might ultimately show His love and mercy to a lost and hurting world.

Acts 10:38 tells "how God anointed Jesus of Nazareth with the Holy Spirit and with power, who went about doing good and healing all who were oppressed by the devil, for God was with Him." God has gifted you and filled you with Himself so that you can be His hands, His feet, His voice in this world. That is why we see the gifts of the Spirit in operation by naturally supernatural people.

The Outcome

We believe that we are seeing a refreshing, a refueling, a refocusing, a re-equipping, a re-stirring of the gifts in the saints of God for the glory of God, for the building up of the Body of Christ, for advancing His Kingdom in power. If you look at the world, it seems as though the darkness is getting darker, but because so many are willing to receive what the Lord has for them the light is also getting lighter.

The first gift opened heaven's treasure-house for all other gifts to come to us. That was the gift of the cosmic intervention of a good God in a world needing redemption. God so loved the world that He gave His only begotten Son that whoever believes in Him will not perish but have eternal life (see John 3:16).

At Calvary God gave: The Father gave the Son; the Son gave Himself; the Spirit gave as Christ's constant companion in every prayer and breath and sigh, with every wound that fell on Jesus to bring us healing.

He truly is the gift that keeps on giving: life, power, refreshing and cleansing. That gift, God's love personally, His life eternally, is the ongoing source of every other gift. Like watching the greatest waterfall, no two moments are the same. And in God we are all invited to drink deeply.

We are reminded of the great story of Israel's deliverance from her miserable years of slavery in Egypt. In one place the Bible records that at a certain moment the whole land was covered with such thick darkness that people could not move from where they sat for three whole days. But it says that where the provision of the Lamb was, in the dwellings of Israel, there was light (see Exodus 10:23).

If you are in a place where you are hungry to get to know the Holy Spirit and desire more clarity about the gifts that He has given you, position yourself in prayer to receive a fresh touch from the Lord and fresh revelation about the supernatural anointing that He has put on your life.

It will be shown in the wisdom He gives, which is higher than human wisdom, the knowledge He gives, which is different from the human way of thinking, the counsel, strategy and understanding He gives, which will help you navigate this life.

Receive a fresh anointing of the grace and peace of God through the Holy Spirit. He will ignite the gifts He has given you, and you will stand with others, a vast community working together for His glory.

Prayer

Lord, You say to earnestly desire spiritual gifts. I am hungry for more of You in my life. I want to hear Your voice and be led by You day by day. I want to flow in more of Your love and supernatural power so that Jesus will be glorified. Help me find my place and purpose in Your Body, and give me wisdom in using Your gifts responsibly. I ask for the gifts of healing, miracles, faith, discerning of spirits, knowledge, wisdom, tongues, interpretation of tongues and prophecy. May I flow in these gifts always yielded to the Holy Spirit, bringing honor to the name of Jesus.

Chapter 9

Power Up

Here is a little exercise. Imagine a candle. Every candle, unless it is improperly made, has a wick running through the middle. You may not see any of the wick but the end of it, but that one little piece is there ready for you to set it on fire.

Now picture this candle as an analogy of a human being and his or her spirit. Just as the wick is able to burn in the candle with fire, so the very fire and light and life of the Spirit of God Himself can become resident in us as human vessels, and we can begin to fulfill our created purpose—notably bearing fruit and using the gifts.

We were created to give light. When our spirits are lit by God's Holy Spirit, we have the potential to shine. In fact, we have the full capacity to know God just as Jesus knew Him when Jesus walked on the earth. That may seem astounding, but it is true. If we are in communion with God, nothing is withheld from us that helps us do the work we were created to do.

We are going to explore in this chapter spiritual things—things of the Holy Spirit of God and the inner spirit part of every human that is waiting to be lit by His Presence.

In order to bear fruit and in order for the gifts God gives us to be fully functioning and effective, we need to understand how this godly partnership works. Until we do, we are likely to have some confusion about matters of spirituality.

Let's start by exploring God's intention for us in Creation, His purpose for making us the way He did.

GOD CREATED US IN HIS IMAGE

The first chapters of the book of Genesis tell us something amazing about ourselves. Scripture makes it clear that God had a plan to make a man and a woman in His own image and that He fulfilled that plan.

Paul uses three terms to encompass the three-part nature of this being God made: spirit, soul and body (see 1 Thessalonians 5:23). This was the perfect "image" of God. But have you ever thought about what it means to be made in His image?

The beginning of our story takes place in a garden. This joyous Creation story says that "the LORD God formed man of the dust of the ground, and breathed into his nostrils the breath of life; and man became a living being" (Genesis 2:7). Our life comes from the breath of God, the *ruach kadesh* of the Holy One, the Holy Spirit. He brought forth the Father's intention in the vessel of clay.

Breathed into his nostrils the breath of life. In the Hebrew those words do not express anything like a gentle puff. The breath was more like an explosive force, an exhalation violent in power. So God from above, initiated from above the work of the Spirit into what He had formed from beneath, the vessel of clay. The light within us burst into flame.

In addition, God provided the man with a soul—the mind, will and emotions—patterned after His own ability to think and feel and desire.

Romans 8:27 says of the Holy Spirit, "He who searches the hearts knows what the mind of the Spirit is." So the Holy Spirit is a rational, thinking Person. Many of His gifts have to do with the mind, will or emotions. And then those gifts enable and empower us in communion with God.

The Bible gives numerous instances of God expressing His thoughts and feelings. Look at the following expression of God, assumed by most theologians to be a picture of the second Person of the Trinity. When the Father formed Adam out of clay and breathed into him the breath of life, there rejoicing with Him was the glorious Son of God, evident here as the wisdom of God:

> "Long before God stretched out Earth's Horizons, and tended to the minute details of Soil and Weather, and set Sky firmly in place, I was there. When he mapped and gave borders to wild Ocean, built the vast vault of Heaven, and installed the fountains that fed Ocean, when he drew a boundary for Sea, posted a sign that said no trespassing, and then staked out Earth's Foundations, I was right there with him, making sure everything fit. Day after day I was there, with my joyful applause, always enjoying his company, delighted with the world of things and creatures, happily celebrating the human family."
>
> Proverbs 8:22–31, THE MESSAGE

Spirit and soul were in the man, patterned after God, but what about the man's body? Does God have a body? Is that part of the image that we reflect? The answer is yes.

Throughout the Old Testament we are given glimpses of the appearances of God—specifically the Son of God. Theologians call this kind of occurrence a *Christophany,* meaning an appearance of the Christ before He actually came to earth as a man.

One example would be the Angel (capital *A*) of the Lord who showed up outside Jericho with a drawn sword when Joshua and the Israelites were preparing to attack the city. Joshua walked up to Him and said, "Sir, which side are you on?" Joshua was a pretty gutsy guy.

And the fellow standing there with His sword said, "Mine. Would you like to be on My side?"

Joshua immediately recognized this was no ordinary human being or even an angel. He fell facedown before the Captain of the Lord's host, the Captain of armies—it was Jesus Himself.

Jesus has always had form. It is a spiritual body, but He has always had it. And He looks like a man. You have arms and legs and a head and a torso because that is a form of how Jesus actually is as the Son of God.

He took on human flesh, however, only when He invested Himself in a human body. This was the incarnation—the overshadowing of Mary by the Holy Spirit when the second Person of the Trinity became a flesh-and-blood Child in her womb.

But here is the particular point we want to recognize. In the initial Creation, God made male and female in His image. He was looking at Jesus and making man similarly. He was envisioning the glory of the Son in whom He took delight, with whom He communed fully and completely. He was reflecting that perfection of delight, the fullness of perpetual joy into the man and woman in the beautiful Garden. God created human beings in a form that reflects how He is—with a body, a soul and a spirit.

It was the Father's desire that just as Jesus and He relate fully to one another with joy inexplicable, so every man, every woman, every child might also be in that fullness of relationship with Him. In this way, the fruit and gifts of the Spirit would be manifested through His communion with our spirits and the yielding of our souls and bodies.

That is how our first parents got created as tripartite beings who walked in fellowship. Sadly, a series of events cut off that joyful communion we had with our Creator.

LIFE IN A FALLEN WORLD

Something happened in our world that deformed the human race, and it happened in that beautiful Garden where the man and woman were created in the image of God.

We believe that the story of Adam and Eve is historically accurate as told in the Bible. Nothing else can answer the great philosophical questions of identity: Who am I? Why am I here? The answers are found in Scripture.

The man and woman were brought to life, lived in a perfect world and walked in perfect harmony with God. Their bodies and minds acted appropriately because their spirits were rightly aligned with His Spirit.

One day, however, with full knowledge of God's warning, they both chose to listen to the voice of deception speaking out of the serpent and ate from the Tree of Knowledge of Good and Evil, which God had forbidden them to do.

You see, the real root of sin is not so much the desire to be evil; it is the desire to be independent from God. When the man and woman under their own volition stepped away from dependence on God, sin and corruption entered the world. At that instant of the Fall, there was a disruption, a break in spiritual communion with God.

Basically Adam and Eve gave precedence to the lust of soul and body. The spirit within them, thus overridden, died. The spirit was not uncreated, so to speak, it was not extinguished, but it was disconnected. The man and woman were now more or less on their own in matters of the spirit and might or might not walk in the ways of wisdom. This is the fallen nature that we each inherit.

God's Plan to Rectify

But thank God, He had another plan. The Lamb was slain before the foundation of the world. From the beginning He knew this would happen and set about to reopen our access to His Spirit. That is why Jesus came. The spirit is regenerated through being born again—a simple act of faith in the Lord Jesus and His work on Calvary; it is a one-time event.

Through it you are regenerated, you are made alive in Christ through His blood. Then as we have seen the Spirit of the Lord comes on you. His manifestation includes the gifts of the Spirit and the fruit of the Spirit. So we look for more fruitfulness and more demonstration of divine power.

God does not impose Himself, but if you say come in and do what you want, He is going to mess up your house. He is going to get out His construction tools, tear out a few walls, install some new plumbing, throw in a little high-grade insulation, new flooring and finally He will hang a few pictures.

He is working on His residence: us.

Or think of yourself as God's garden. You are His garden of delight, the paradise of God! Does that make you happy inside? He longs for us to be fully aware, walking in this knowledge moment by moment. We are that important to Him.

God is perfect all in Himself, but when He lost communion with humankind, He was missing something that He set His heart and mind to recover: His garden of paradise with us.

He had us in mind specifically, by name. He knew all about us.

He had everything in His mind, in His heart, in His book before the moment of conception. That is pretty significant when you realize your life is more than just a span of years on this earth. For God, you existed even prior to conception.

King David observed this marvel in one of his psalms: "In Your book they all were written, the days fashioned for me, when as yet there were none of them" (Psalm 139:16). The Lord told this to Jeremiah. He said, "Before I formed you in the womb I knew you" (Jeremiah 1:5). That is pretty fantastic; that is pretty marvelous. That should help us if we are ever having any kind of identity crisis.

God had something in mind. His intention was that our spirits would be reawakened, be reborn, be born again from death, sin and corruption. Thus He sent His Son, Jesus, into the fallen world to redeem it by His life. Fully human yet fully divine, Jesus died in our place on the cross, defeated the devil and opened the way for us to have full restoration with the Father.

When we ask the risen Lord to make His home in our hearts by the power of the Holy Spirit, our spirits are changed. They are brought to that new life. If Christ is in you, then when the Father looks at you or thinks of you, it is with exactly the same fullness of the joy that He had with the Son in the beginning and that He has with Him now.

Our spirits are made new; the "wicks" are aligned and burn brightly. When the Holy Spirit fills—and refills—us with His power, we can live our lives with spiritual grace and anointing.

Our bodies and souls, however, still need work! If there is any barrier in receiving that fullness of Spirit experientially, it is probably lodging in one of the two other parts of our makeup—in our human bodies or in our souls.

The devil still exists, and his kingdom continues in opposition to God's Kingdom. Spirituality is a connection with the invisible realities of one or the other of those kingdoms.

Many, many people are deeply seeking to make a connection with invisible things that are counter to God. They pursue these not only through sensory perception, but also through the soul's ability to conjure them up. The devil is more than glad to influence the body and the soul. We have choices to make in these areas.

The Human Body

The body is *world-conscious*. It is in contact with physical, elemental things through the senses. As a world-conscious entity, the body responds primarily to pleasure or pain.

Our bodies were created by God to be vessels for both soul and spirit. They enable us to perform the will of God. When Paul calls the body a "temple," he is indicating the holy nature of God's Presence in us. Our bodies are a place for the life-giving Spirit to dwell.

Think about it for a minute. Your body is a temple. It has a purpose. It does not matter what it looks like, how big, little, twisted or straight it is, what color it is or how it smells. We have bodies for God's glory.

As temples for the Holy Spirit, our bodies are redeemed, cleansed and sanctified by the blood of Jesus. The members of the body—our eyes, our ears, our hands, our tongues, our hearts and every other part—are intended to be instruments for righteousness.

Why do you have a body? To praise the Lord! Under the divine influence of the Spirit of God, our bodies can carry out His divine pleasure in the earth. You can see the difference between this and the "fallen" kind of worldview that says, "I am here to seek my own pleasure—to feed this body, dress it, adorn it, modify it."

The Human Soul

As we have noted, the soul includes the mind, will and emotions. In other words, the soul is *self-conscious*. As with the body's choices, that can be a good thing or it can be a bad thing. If we are focused on nothing else except what *we* think, what *we* feel, what *we* want, then we are not fulfilling the purposes of God.

Here is the problem. Because of the Fall and the deadening of the spirit within us, our human perception, and therefore our experience of God, is based only on what we can perceive with our minds. Left to ourselves, the soul can move in partnership with the body in a way that can lead to trouble, or, at the least, not necessarily be all that productive.

When the Bible talks about being carnal (see Colossians 3:3, for instance), it is not necessarily talking about sin, it is talking about the illumination that you can get if you only have natural sensory perception giving you that knowledge.

Being carnally minded is being human minded, and it is at odds with the things of God (see Romans 8:6–7). The human mind on its own cannot perceive or receive the knowledge of God. Only through the Holy Spirit can that knowledge be given.

This is a great privilege for Christians, but also we should realize that it puts great responsibility on us. We have an obligation, because we have been awakened to what it means to be truly human.

The good news is, God takes pleasure in our souls and bodies. The bad news is our experience of them is a work in progress, and it does take discipline.

The Human Spirit

The spirit is God-conscious. People can talk about God-consciousness all that they want, but if they have not encountered the Living God, whose name is Jesus, they have no true sense of who He is.

Jesus asked Peter a vital question, "Who do you say I am?" All of the philosophical and religious answers in the world, all of the traditional pop culture theories, every personal speculation meant nothing at that moment.

Peter confessed the truth: "You are the Christ, the Son of the living God."

Jesus told him where that answer came from: "You didn't get that from your soul—the part that says *I want, I think, I feel.* You didn't get it from your body, your five senses and the fact that you can see Me and we can eat together. No, something happened in your spirit. Your spirit was one with the Father, and that is how you knew the truth."

He is who He says He is. And when He comes by the Spirit your spirit is made alive, and there is union there. That is why the Bible tells us not to grieve the Holy Spirit. It cuts off your fruitfulness, your productivity, your life.

SPIRIT WORSHIP

We read in John's gospel the story of Jesus talking to a woman at a well who was very religious. She was telling Him all about her understanding of spiritual things, and He then said, "Let Me tell you how it works. God seeks true worshipers—those who worship Him in spirit and in truth."

Our starting point on the subject of spirituality reminds us that God desires a people who are in harmony with Him and, therefore, reflect His image and His glory in heaven. The only way to do that is by having access to God Himself by the Spirit of God.

> For who among men knows the thoughts of a man except the man's spirit within him? In the same way no one knows the thoughts of God except the Spirit of God. We have not received the spirit of the world but the Spirit who is from God, that we may understand what God has freely given us. This is what we speak, not in words taught us by human wisdom but in words taught by the Spirit, expressing spiritual truths in spiritual words. The man without the Spirit does not accept the things that come from the Spirit of God, for they are foolishness to him, and he cannot understand them, because they are spiritually discerned. The spiritual man makes judgments about all things, but he himself is not subject to any man's judgment: "For who has known the mind of the Lord that he may instruct him?" But we have the mind of Christ.

1 Corinthians 2:11–16, NIV

First Corinthians 2:9–10 gives this insight: " 'Eye has not seen, nor ear heard, nor have entered into the heart of man the things which God has prepared for those who love Him.' But God has revealed them to us through His Spirit." God is spirit; it is only possible to worship God by the Spirit of God.

Worship has a function, an end game. What is it meant to do? Worship is meant to bring us into fellowship with God. When we enter that kind of friendship we have fuller revelation, fuller knowledge of God.

In other words, He shares His secrets with us. The Holy Spirit gives revelation to us that is beyond the natural seeing eye, the natural hearing ear, the natural thinking mind.

Do you see the progression? Worship brings friendship; God reveals His secrets to His friends; His friends get greater revelation.

We see there the fullness of God's plan. Through the sacrifice of the Lord Jesus Christ and the Presence of the Holy Spirit, we once again have full access to the fullness of God.

We are all living in the world, and we are part of what is going on all around us. We have things to do, people to see, places to visit. But if that is all we are doing, we are missing out on the point of living. The point is to respond to the heart of God and be conformed to the likeness of Jesus, who is the image of the invisible One. Our quest in this life is the ecstasy of communion that can never be broken. This is not religiosity. It is real spirituality, and there is a difference.

A young woman named Kelly told us how she was struggling with the idea of a relationship with God. She was taking a class at a Christian college and listened one day as others described how they sensed the closeness of Jesus.

"I was hearing people say things like: 'Jesus and I are so close' and 'Jesus and I walked through the park' and 'Jesus and I did this and we did that.' And I was sitting there thinking, *Where is He? I don't feel Him at all.*

"I came home in tears," she said. "I told a friend who was visiting, 'I hate this class. I don't know why I did this. I can't even get my money back.' I just didn't understand. To tell you the truth, I felt as though I was in marriage counseling with Jesus; the relationship just was not working."

Since she could not get a refund, she decided to finish the course. One night she suddenly realized that she was disappointed with God and what had and had not happened in her life.

As she was able to open herself honestly, she was able to hear the Holy Spirit speaking to her for the first time. He brought the words of a song to her mind—a love song—and things "clicked." She realized that the Holy Spirit is not only a Person, but a Person who loves her.

Many individuals like Kelly know a lot of things in their heads, but have less awareness in their hearts. Yet it is in the inner person that we experience the fullness of who the Holy Spirit is. Once you respond to His voice drawing you into His presence, He takes you higher into the presence of the Living God, and you experience more and more fulfillment, and more and more glory, more and more beauty.

Think of it as if you are really two "people." There is the outward person, the one you present to others, and then there is the hidden person, the "real you" in the heart. There is usually an aspect of that hidden person that, no matter how intimate you get with another human being, you always reserve some things because they are too precious to you to lay out there in public. You keep them in a private room and lock the door.

This is what we all need to know: God loves that room. He wants that room. He desires that room and the parts of that inner you that are broken, afraid, empty, void, disheveled, ruined, hurt, sensitive, tender or whatever—that part of you that is never shared for reasons of shame or intimidation or fear of rejection.

The Holy Spirit loves both "yous." He loves and accepts the face you present to others, and He also knows and desires to be allowed to settle down in the hidden you, the heart person. Every heart has a voice; the voice of the Lord is the Holy Spirit speaking to our hearts. Just as the human heart sings, imagines, weeps, yearns, withdraws and takes courage, all of those things are reflections of the divine personality and work and ministry and presence of the Holy Spirit in us.

So potentially, then, we can live in harmony with Someone who is complete when we feel bound by limitation. He will sing with us. He will weep with us. He will imagine with us. He will yearn with us. And when we withdraw, He will draw aside with us, but He will not draw away.

Jesus told us that the Holy Spirit will come to everyone who receives Him. The Holy Spirit will come as helper, teacher, comforter, guide, counselor, advocate. In the original Greek, one of His names is Parakletos, "the One who comes and fills the empty place beside." And once He comes, as long as you want Him, He will never leave you.

The Breath of God

The spirit in you that has been made alive in Christ, that has been born again, that has become a new creation by the breath of God will—along with your soul—live forever. Let that sink in for a minute: You are never going to die. You will abide with God forever.

When you consider that, what is there to be afraid of? When you face difficulties, which the Bible calls "momentary light afflictions," will you let them oppress and torment your spirit, your mind, your body?

Consider them tests that purify the divine life of Christ that is in you until all the wood, hay and stubble, all the soulishness, all the carnality, all the natural thinking and natural living toward this world have suddenly burned away, and that wick in you shines ever more brightly. It is Christ in you, and it is glorious.

Prayer

Father, You knew me before I was formed in my mother's womb. You know my thoughts before I speak. Because of the precious blood of Your Son, Jesus, You are with me and in me always by Your Spirit. I want to know You. Awaken my heart to love Your presence more every day. May I hunger to know You through Your Word. May I grow closer to my Friend, the Holy Spirit, day by day. I invite You to search my heart and remove anything that would hinder my knowing You. May I burn brightly with Your fire, and be a light showing Your love and power to the world around me.

Chapter 10

Mirror Image

We are on a journey, and our destination is to commune with the Holy Spirit, to cooperate with Him and His work in our lives. To state it most concisely, the Holy Spirit is holy; it is His desire to make us holy as well. The Lord's intention is that we live in complete health—body, soul and spirit. Then we, being whole, can minister that wholeness to others.

Does holiness seem too great a challenge? Most of us come to Jesus wounded, defeated, lost or broken. Thankfully we recognize that it is His ministry, His work past and present, that equips us for holy living.

So how do we achieve inner harmony by which every part of us is dancing to one tune, and that tune is the will of the Holy Spirit? How do we enter that place of righteousness, peace and joy?

Christians are members of a new supernatural race, though for the time being we dwell in corruptible mortal bodies. Paul says that the body, soul and spirit, those three aspects of our makeup, will be preserved blameless—in other words, completely redeemed and made whole and healthy until the coming of the Lord. When we see Jesus at His return, "we will be like Him." Imagine that!

That is exciting. Until then, we look to the Holy Spirit to help us be holy.

THE SEARCH FOR PERFECTION

We cannot become holy unless we are willing to deal with sin. Sin, which often has some basis in woundedness, is not just doing bad things; it is a state of being that has imperfection as it relates to the perfection of God.

And what is the perfection of the Holy Spirit? He is love. He is righteousness, peace and joy. The fruit of the Spirit is gentleness, goodness, kindness—He exudes, emanates and radiates perfection.

As He draws us in, His radiating perfection sheds light on what is present deep inside us. Someone wounded you deeply when you were three? You began to steal when you were fifteen? You have never dealt with the sin that has taken hold of your heart? Darkness cannot hide in His presence. True worship demands a true assessment of sin.

One day Jesus went to meet a woman at a well. She was a Samaritan woman; the Jewish people of Jesus' day looked down on Samaritans as inferior. In addition, she had had five husbands. There is no telling what was really going on in her life.

But Jesus went out of His way to meet her. He did not respond to her according to the religious façade that she presented. He did not respond to her on the basis that she probably had it together on the outside. No, He went straight to the heart. He looked right through all that façade, to the broken place inside, to bring healing to her.

And when He spoke to her inner person, she suddenly got illumination and saw her state. That illumination opened the way for complete healing. She was healed that day. She was delivered, and she went immediately and brought all of her broken friends and said, "Come see the Man who healed me. He told me everything about myself and brought me to total inner harmony."

Jeremiah said, "My heart [my inner man] within me is broken ... all my bones shake" (Jeremiah 23:9). The word *heart* in Scripture refers to the deepest, innermost part of every human. This verse shows us that there is a connection between the spirit and the physical members of our bodies.

Physical health is very much dependent on inner wholeness; physical sickness can be related to anything that suppresses the work of the Holy Spirit in our lives. Sinfulness has an impact upon our souls, and this usually affects our bodies as well.

It is the Holy Spirit's desire that we be sinless, so that wholeness can radiate out to the soul and body.

When John wrote these words, "Beloved, I pray that you may prosper in all things and be in health, just as your soul prospers" (3 John 1:2), he was talking about more than just the body being in health. Again we see a connection between the inner man and the outer man. If we look at the original Greek, the essence of that greeting in John's letter is something like this:

> Favorite friends, worthy of love, I pray to God regarding everything that concerns you, that you might have a direct and easy path to success, with soundness, good health, strength of grace in your soul, the seat of your desires, affections, feelings and aversions.

This prayer for a sense of harmony that comes from God was not a general wish of John's. He was praying that spiritual health would burst out into every aspect of the lives of the believers.

Let's look more closely at holiness as the Holy Spirit's work in us.

GAZING IN HIS MIRROR

There is a story in the Bible about the time that Israel was building the Tabernacle in the wilderness. God had given Moses the plans for the place where His Living Presence would come to reside. God had both led and come behind the whole nation enabling and providing for them as they made their way to the land He had promised to give them as their own possession.

As Israel was delivered from Egypt by great miracles, their former captors sent them away with all kinds of treasure! As God gave the blueprint for His "house on wheels," the Tabernacle, the people of Israel freely gave those treasures to be used in building the place where they would have fellowship with Him.

In the same way, God has designed you as His own piece of creative genius to show forth an aspect of His beauty and wonder. As you receive Christ, He gives you gifts and your Best Friend installs and activates them for display and use in every aspect of your life. You are His treasure, and He fills you with His Spirit who carries all God's heavenly treasure so you become a valuable vessel in fellowship with God day to day.

The women of Israel donated the mirrors they had been using to see their reflection and improve their appearance. Those mirrors were melted down and formed into a great washbasin. It was filled with fresh water every day, and the priests washed there making themselves ready to enter the tent of God's Presence and talk with Him face-to-face.

It pointed to a coming metamorphosis: our self-image for God's. For all those who did not like what they had seen looking back at them, what a blessing! What a healing! What a mind-shift! This is exactly what Jesus made possible for each of us through His death, burial, resurrection and outpouring of the Spirit.

The Bible is the mirror the Spirit uses to reflect our inner person. When we look in it, things in us that are not apparent to the human eye may be revealed. It shows who we are and where we are in relationship to God. It will never lie to us. It is the only book in the world that is living. When we read it, it is actually reading us. And the Author is right there looking over our shoulders encouraging, directing, correcting and leading us along.

As we look into this mirror, we see Jesus' image is looking back out from it. He is gazing right into our hearts and something supernatural is going on. A miracle is taking place. A flawless mirror is revealing a flawless Person. His reflection is changing everyone who gazes on Him regularly and long enough.

There is no more need to hide behind masks or under cover of darkness: For "we all, with unveiled face, beholding as in a mirror the glory of the Lord, are being transformed into the same image from glory to glory, just as by the Spirit of the Lord" (2 Corinthians 3:18).

This mirror reveals the glories, the beauty, majesty, the wonder, love, grace, generosity, forgiveness, wealth, praise, kindness and on and on of Jesus. It is like what happens when you stand between two mirrors and your reflection goes on into infinity. We see Jesus' infinite goodness.

And through Jesus' loving look back in our direction, the Holy Spirit is working busily on our hearts. He is cutting away the flesh of our former selves. He will keep working until He has finished the makeover, and the one gazing back at Jesus in the mirror will be someone with His exact nature and glory.

THE RIGHT VIEW OF HOLINESS

There is a perfect framework that came out of God's being when He spoke, and the Holy Spirit hovered and the worlds were made. It is called "moral law." People tend to start getting nervous, especially if you are talking about religious things, and you bring up "law."

But it is interesting that we turn readily to law in our natural everyday lives if someone commits some act of injustice against us. We want the law to come to our side, stand up for our part, make things right and repay or compensate us for what we suffered or lost.

The impulse toward wanting things put right when we have been wronged comes from the eternal, perfect, "holy" nature of God that stands behind order in the universe and keeps things from literally turning into unimaginable chaos.

We are actually talking about "holiness." The Holy Spirit is holy. Because *He is*, there exists a true difference between good and evil, right and wrong, darkness and light, justice and injustice, life and death. His existence as holy is behind all good; it is the reason we have a future and hope!

That is what salvation is. We exchange our missing the mark of all that is good, light, just and right for Jesus' goodness, light, eternal life and perfect justice. It is the exchange of "unholiness" for holiness. This explains why salvation is both good news and an unmerited gift that only God can give. There is no way to receive it except by turning away from darkness back to God.

The heart is deceitful and set on actively corrupting you if it is left without the power of Christ's exchange on the cross: "The heart is deceitful above all things, and desperately wicked; who can know [who can cure] it?" (Jeremiah 17:9).

Your old deceitful trickster heart is always trying to get away with going its own way, doing its own thing, refusing to give up and turn itself in for a life of freedom in the captive love of God.

So what do you do to get out of such a mess? With your mind and will you make a decision as God faithfully comes to you by the Holy Spirit bringing His gift of grace to turn you around and point you toward the life of God and the Person who is the truth, Jesus, the Anointed One.

Even Paul, the great miracle-working, fearless, tireless, willing bond servant of God said, "There's a war going on inside me! Can anyone deliver me from this miserable dilemma? Why, yes! Only One. I thank my God He has done it through the perfect Son, Jesus!"

And John wrote about the new heart given to everyone who receives Jesus:

> Those who have been born into God's family do not make a practice of sinning, because God's life is in them. So they can't keep on sinning, because they are children of God. So now we can tell who are children of God and who are children of the devil. Anyone who does not live righteously and does not love other believers does not belong to God.
>
> 1 John 3:9–10, NLT

The Spirit of holiness is the only One able to give you the power you need for this new life as a child of God.

> We know that God's children do not make a practice of sinning, for God's Son holds them securely, and the evil one cannot touch them. We know that we are children of God and that the world around us is under the control of the evil one. And we know that the Son of God has come, and he has given us understanding so that we can know the true God. And now we live in fellowship

with the true God because we live in fellowship with his Son, Jesus Christ. He is the only true God, and he is eternal life. Dear children, keep away from anything that might take God's place in your hearts.

1 John 5:18–21, NLT

So how do you do it? Surely there must be a law because rules and regulations are the first thing we turn to if we think about being holy.

Did you know that the Jewish traditions hold everything about the Law of God and all its statutes in the Old Testament as blessings? They get excited about the challenge of keeping each of them day to day.

They are called *mitzvoth*, connection, meaning keeping you connected to God. The commandments are connectors because each one reflects a bit of God's moral perfection. They don't make God holy, but each rule or regulation makes a distinction between what is right and what is not right. Each of them reflects a little idea that God is light and right and has no wrong or darkness in Him.

That is what holiness means—wholly excellent, gloriously pure, completely majestic and delightfully, deliciously wonderful in every way, with absolutely nothing in Him that could mess it all up in any way no matter what.

And He wants to walk with us? Forever?

Would anyone really want to turn down such a deal? Say yes to Jesus, and the whole package is yours all at once.

WHERE WE WENT ASTRAY

So, let's put this business of holiness in the right perspective by using that Law, the first agreement God made with Israel, the people

He chose to be His special nation on earth. He said something that is plain common sense and each of us experiences this regularly: "Can two people walk together without agreeing on the direction?" (Amos 3:3, NLT).

Good question. The verse before that one says: "From among all the families on the earth, I have been intimate with you alone. That is why I must punish you for all your sins." You are probably saying, "There you go. I knew it! Bring up holiness and you drag sin into the conversation, in particular my sin. Conversation over."

Think of it this way. God views His relationship with us like a marriage. He is the husband, and we are His wife. He went looking for a bride and chose us to live happily ever after together with Him. There is just one problem: We are not perfect like He is. That puts us all in a position to wander off from time to time wanting to shack up with a stranger.

Let's call him Mr. Sin. And he is a rascal who totally misses the mark if you are aiming at the bull's-eye of being like Jesus and agreeing with God about everything.

But you (and we) made your choice and had an affair with Mr. Sin and by doing so, broke your marriage vows. Maybe you didn't mean it. Maybe you wish now you had not done it. But trickster heart thought it was fine while the affair with sin was going on. It seemed fun. It felt fine. It just ended badly, and when you woke up alone you wanted to go home and be welcomed with open arms, all forgiven as if nothing had happened.

You wanted God to take you back and forget about it. To treat you as if nothing had come between you and get right back to happily ever after. Problem is, after sleeping around with sin you have changed. You find that now, every once in a while, the shadow of guilt or shame or the memory of what went on creeps up and bullies you around. The old lover turns up on the doorstep even when you keep telling him to leave you alone. That is what the apostle Paul meant when he said, "Who will deliver me from this mess? Thank God, He has through Jesus."

Jesus made the switch and gave us His heart as the trade-in for our old one. He did that on the cross. As He was sacrificing Himself He asked God to go ahead and level every bit of punishment on Him that justice demands of injustice, light demands of darkness and good demands of evil.

Holy God meted it out, and perfect Jesus paid it in full. Then He died and took all our missing the mark to the grave with Him and buried it there. That is why something supernatural happens when you are water baptized. The old trickster heart dies, and gone with it are all the old relations with Mr. Sin and his crowd.

You get up out of the grave as a brand-new God-lover ready to walk with Him as His faithful partner. The undeserved favor of God offers it, and the Spirit of holiness does the operation from start to finish.

We have His clear instructions. He told Moses, "Give the following instructions to the entire community of Israel. You must be holy because I, the LORD your God, am holy" (Leviticus 19:2, NLT).

How? "You shall keep My statutes. Behave in such a way that it's plain for all to see that we are married. I belong to you, you belong to Me and there's no third party in our bed. Neither one of us is keeping a lover on the side." That's holiness.

If the human race had stuck to its vows, we would have remained pure. But we free-thinking folks decided to do it our own way instead. Thus, the only thing we had left was a rule book to show where we had gone wrong and how to get back.

Perhaps this is why people think holiness is a set of rules. Holiness has to do with who God is and what He is like by nature.

God is holy. He does not have a checklist of things He has to do and things He must not do every day in order to be holy. Holiness is a summation of the divine characteristics of God Himself.

UNDERSTANDING HOLINESS

Jesus said, "I am the way, the truth and the life." We do not normally think of a "way" as a person. Generally we imagine a "way" as a thing like a physical path or an idea, like a certain manner of doing something. But God is different. He Himself, the Person, is the way.

What way? The only way to know your heavenly Father. The only way to have forgiveness and eternal life. Yes, those things are true, but the way in God's case is not a thing but a Person.

God has various names by which He is called in Scripture: "Lord," "the God of Abraham, Isaac and Jacob," "the Rock of Israel" and a number of names given as He revealed Himself in some mighty act like "God our Peace," when He came to Gideon, or the "Captain of Armies" when He met Joshua at Jericho.

Job was a righteous man by human standards. When he had a revelation of the Lord he said, "I repent in dust and ashes. I abhor myself." There is the revelation of the difference between God's holiness and the best we can do.

That is why holiness is not a set of good works. Holiness is the impartation of God in whatever measure we receive it. Approaching Him is the same as a trusting child going to sit in Papa's lap: We know He wants us, and that is where we are safe and happy. The more we can relax the better it is.

If holiness is who God is by His mere "being-ness," then what are some of the things God is?

God is light. "In Him is no darkness at all" (1 John 1:5).

God is love. "And we have known and believed the love that

God has for us. God is love, and he who abides in love abides in God, and God in him" (1 John 4:16).

God is upright. That does not mean uptight! "For I proclaim the name of the LORD: Ascribe greatness to our God. He is the Rock, His work is perfect; for all His ways are justice, a God of truth and without injustice; righteous and upright is He" (Deuteronomy 32:3–4).

God is eternally merciful. "Praise the LORD! Oh, give thanks to the LORD, for He is good! For His mercy endures forever" (Psalm 106:1).

God is mighty. "The LORD on high is mightier than the noise of many waters, than the mighty waves of the sea" (Psalm 93:4).

And God is holy. "Holy, Holy, Holy is the LORD of hosts; the whole earth is full of His glory!" (Isaiah 6:1).

The realization that God is indeed holy shakes every false foundation. His holiness is like a plumb line a carpenter uses to set a wall straight.

His Unique State

God is unique in His holiness. And we can only understand or become partakers of holiness insofar as we relate to God as He is. He is unable to compromise at all in terms of anything untrue or evil or dark. The wrong way of thinking or doing something will not mix with who God is. It is like water and oil—by their very components they separate when they are put together in the same vessel.

Missing the mark is called by the word *sin* in the Bible. It helps us to get a more proper grasp on what holiness is and is not. Because Jesus gave us the clothing of His character, Hebrews 12:14 tells us to go for it: "Pursue peace with all people, and holiness, without which no one will see the Lord." Run after God's holiness with all your strength. Keep the mirror in front of you and realize He is making you like Him as you do.

The Concept of Zeal

There is another feature of God's holy being that cannot be overlooked in our discussion. God is "zealous."

An illustration from Jesus' life is the day He went into the Temple and set things back on their proper foundation. He threw out the money changers and said, "This place was built for prayer!" The disciples remembered that zeal for God's house would consume Him.

In Old English it is the word *jealous,* meaning "completely devoted to something with your whole personality to such a degree that you are unwilling to part with that object of your affection." You will go to great lengths to secure and keep it all for yourself only.

A few years ago a certain celebrity told a large audience how as a child sitting in church she heard the preacher read these words from the Bible: "I the Lord am a jealous God." This woman's comment was, "I don't want anything to do with a God who's like that."

What a tragedy that she was given no counsel or understanding about what those words reveal about God! Because of her wrong assumptions, she shut all the doors to true fulfillment, as was evident in the things she chose to seek with her time and money.

When the Lord said, "I the Lord am a jealous God," He was revealing that it is His full nature to be all about an "other." He is the Father to His child, the Groom to His Bride, the big Brother to His little brother, the Shepherd to His lambs—all of those things and more. He is zealously seeking every human being.

Every person wants to be wanted, and what more beauteous

truth than to discover you are wanted by the One who is beauty Himself? That is amazing. And that is why we receive Him, we welcome Him, we honor Him, we appreciate Him.

"Since we are receiving a kingdom which cannot be shaken, let us have grace, by which we may serve God acceptably with reverence and godly fear. For our God is a consuming fire" (Hebrews 12:28–29).

This, too, is an aspect of God's holy zeal. When God gets mad it is righteous. Jesus was mad as hornets stirred up when He saw what had become of Israel's sanctuary of worship. That fire purifies what is good and makes it even purer and more valuable until it is very precious in God's sight. That fire burns up everything that opposes God or refuses to walk in peace with Him.

A New Perspective

Now we can see that holiness is something much more than a negative attitude of trying to stop sinning and keep yourself clean by observing rules and regulations. Holiness is becoming a being whose composite nature is holy.

The Holy Spirit was holy before sin entered the universe, and He will be holy when sin has been banished forever. We are made partakers of His eternal nature. Paul told the Christians living in Rome, the then "sin-capital" of the world:

> By the mercies of God . . . present your bodies a living sacrifice, holy, acceptable to God, which is your reasonable service. And do not be conformed to this world, but be transformed by the renewing of your mind, that you may prove what is that good and acceptable and perfect will of God.
>
> Romans 12:1–2

The mirror does it.

It changes our whole way of thinking. As we gaze into the Word of God, it washes us inside and makes a difference in us between what is holy and what is not.

We start thinking differently. We start thinking like the Holy Spirit. Then our actions begin to reflect His behavior as well. Suddenly we are walking together in perfect step with Him and He with us.

This is that process the Bible calls being sanctified, made holy, set apart to God for His holy purpose: "For whom He [God] foreknew, He also predestined to be conformed to the image of His Son, that He might be the firstborn among many brethren" (Romans 8:29).

Peter summed it up this way:

> [God's] divine power has given to us all things that pertain to life and godliness, through the knowledge of Him who called us by glory and virtue, by which have been given to us exceedingly great and precious promises, that through these you may be partakers of the divine nature, having escaped the corruption that is in the world through lust.
>
> 2 Peter 1:3–4

The power of the Holy Spirit provides us with all that we need to live a holy life. Avail yourself, pursue and let Him overtake you!

THE PROMISE OF GOD

There is a wonderful story in the book of 2 Samuel (9:1–13) that shows the provision of the Holy Spirit that God intends for us.

A young man named Mephibosheth, who was crippled as a child, is living in a city named *Lo Debar*. Lo Debar means a place of no pasture. It is barren.

Mephibosheth is actually of royal blood, for he was the grandson of Israel's first king, King Saul. But most of Saul's household is dead. By this point in the story David has been crowned king.

Many of us have been living like Mephibosheth in Lo Debar. We have thought, *Healing is not for us. Miracles are not for us. The gifts of the Spirit are not for us today. God doesn't answer prayer. We have to suffer through this oppression.* We think we are forced to live in isolation in Lo Debar.

We fail to believe God when He says, "You are not supposed to be living in barrenness and fruitlessness. You are a royal priesthood, a holy nation. You are anointed."

Now King David had a covenant with Mephibosheth's father, Jonathan. David and Jonathan were devoted friends, and David was very grieved when Jonathan was killed in a battle with one of Israel's enemies. So one day he asked one of his officers, "How can I bless Jonathan's inheritance? Is there anybody alive of Jonathan's family?"

A servant of Saul's household was brought to the king and told him, "There is a boy named Mephibosheth who is lame in both feet living in Lo Debar." They brought Mephibosheth to the king, and he was trembling, terrified that the king wanted to kill him. How many times do people fail to come to the Lord because they are terrified that He is mad and going to demolish them?

If God wants to help you develop and grow, He will do so gently. If you have had surgery you know how they put you under the anesthesia. Then you awaken and say, "What happened?" And the doctor explains that the cartilage in your knee had degenerated or whatever procedure he did while you were sleeping.

God is better than any surgeon. He is a Father who loves you.

So poor Mephibosheth was brought terrified into the king's presence, and the king said, "No, I loved your father. Everything that belonged to him I am giving to you. And you will eat always here at my table." One other interesting note: Mephibosheth was lame in both his feet. But in Jewish custom, meals were eaten in a reclining position. People would not have noticed his legs.

We may come to God and say, "Lord, I messed up. I have done this. I have done that. I have done so much to offend You."

And God says, "No, you belong to Jesus. I want you here to dine with us." It does not matter that you come to Him lame or bruised or broken. It is all under the blood of Jesus because you belong to Him.

So today move from Lo Debar. Today be free from all condemnation. Today take the hand of the Friend who loves you. All the promises of God are in Him.

Climbing Higher

The patriarch Jacob (whose name means "trickster") had received the promise that he would inherit all his father's wealth and blessing. One night in the desert, with only a rock for a pillow, Jacob dreamed about a ladder that went from where he was on earth right up to where God sits on His heavenly throne.

Our spiritual mentor used to say that that ladder is found in God's Word. Its foot is set on earth, but its head reaches to heaven— the plane of God's being. Each rung in that ladder is a promise. As we plant our hands and feet of faith upon the promises of God's Word, we lift ourselves up out of the earthly realm and closer to the heavenly realm. As we claim God's promises, each one lifts us higher above earth's corruption and puts another measure of God's nature in us.

The life of holiness is the continual, active laying hold, hand over hand, on each rung of that ladder, up, up, up.

Find those promises. Memorize them. Declare them. Say them out loud over yourself and your family, your business and your livestock and pets. Confess those words of God right out in the atmosphere around you. Settle on them as your foundation. Build on them day by day. With every promise you are climbing higher by the power of the Spirit.

Your friend the Holy Spirit is helping you go higher every day as you relate to Him. If you want to be the friend and, more, God's mate for eternity, you want to make the Spirit whose first name is Holy at home where you are in everything you are doing.

GUIDELINES FOR CLIMBING

Here are some steps that can take you higher.

1. Present your body as a sacrifice on God's altar. The altar is the cross of Christ. It sanctifies all who become personally identified with Him there.

2. Refuse to imitate or follow the way of the world and its latest passion. This world and everything in it is constantly changing and all the while it is passing away. When the going seems to get tough, and you feel as though you are the only one going against the flow, remember: "No temptation has overtaken you except such as is common to man; but God is faithful, who will not allow you to be tempted beyond what you are able, but with the temptation will also make the way of escape, that you may be able to bear it" (1 Corinthians 10:13). "And God is able to make all grace abound toward you, that you, always having all

sufficiency in all things, may have an abundance for every good work" (2 Corinthians 9:8).

3. Renew your mind. You have been given the mind of Christ (see 1 Corinthians 2:16) so you are enabled to think God's thoughts and evaluate situations the way He does.

4. Pursue the acceptable will, the good will and the perfect will of God for you. Refuse to settle for anything short of perfect!

5. Be happy! God sits in the heavens and laughs (see Psalm 2:4). Be happy even in the face of your enemies because up there where God sits He is laughing in victory for you over all the forces working against you.

6. Love. John is called the beloved disciple. No wonder he talks so much about the love of God in his writings. Here is just one: "He who has My commandments and keeps them, it is he who loves Me" (John 14:21). We see that to love is to obey, to obey is to love. Love that is true embraces and speaks the truth. Love that is true makes a distinction between what is good and what is not. Love prevails because it forgives in the face of the truth. Love is perfect. True love is holy and holiness is ultimately expressed through love that is true.

7. Worship Him because He is holy! "The LORD reigns; let the peoples tremble! He dwells between the cherubim; let the earth be moved! The LORD is great in Zion, and He is high above all the peoples. Let them praise Your great and awesome name—He is holy" (Psalm 99:1–3).

SPIRIT TO SPIRIT

In the book of Revelation we get insight about the face-to-face communion we will have one day with God: "I looked, and behold, a door standing open in heaven. And the first voice which I heard was like a trumpet speaking with me, saying, 'Come up here'" (Revelation 4:1).

Our bodies are here and not yet in Jesus' actual presence in heaven, but one of the powerful truths of being a Christian is that our spirits are present with God by the Holy Spirit. We are actually in two places at one time! We are on earth, and if we are born again, we are also in heaven communing with the Father and the Son. Our Best Friend makes this possible. He helps us to know God as intimately as God knows us, hour by hour, day by day.

This is the amazing majestic act that the Holy Spirit continues to do in our lives. As we commune with God by the Spirit He is also sculpting us, literally transforming us into the likeness of Jesus in every way. It all boils down to love, alive and active. And don't forget, ultimately in the resurrection we will each have a glorious, eternal body, too.

Love is the ultimate liberty. If God can so work love in us, there is nothing that can happen that can separate us from that abiding assurance. Love suddenly resolves every relational conflict because no matter how people are treating you, you are free in the sense that your response is love. Same with peace. No matter what is going on, we are walking around in what the Bible calls *shalom*, wholeness, blessed assurance that our ultimate end in everything is for good and for glory.

All of these things are the outworking, the fruit of the presence of the high priestly ministry of Jesus made real to us by the Person of the Holy Spirit.

When God told John to "come up here," he did. "At once [John] was in the spirit," and in the literal presence of God in heaven he saw things, heard things, experienced realities that are eternal. When you are in the Spirit you have spiritual eyes and spiritual ears that enable you to see and hear in dimensions beyond merely natural ones.

We cannot see this place of the Spirit with our natural eyes. It is deeper than our current minds and bodies can comprehend. But when our spirits are alive in Christ, the manifest Presence of God dwells there just the same. He bypasses our mind, will and emotions to speak to us. When you learn to recognize it, you bring your mind and body into His will. God wants to awaken our spirits to "come up here" and be in conversation with Him. He wants us awakened to experience that other dimension now. To literally live in heaven on earth.

Everything about the Bible is personal. It points to the Person of God Almighty and it points to the persons He is in communion with. When you have the peace of God, the fear of people does not prevent you from holy living.

John, in his visit in heaven, saw God seated on the throne surrounded by a brilliant rainbow. The beauty of Jesus shining in all His glory and strength creates the appearance of this rainbow. Jesus said the Holy Spirit would come to be in us and with us as Christ Himself. That means when we are fully awakened to acknowledge and commune with our Friend, the Holy Spirit, there is an atmosphere of heaven, like that beautiful rainbow, surrounding us at all times in every situation.

John also saw a sea like glass extending from Jesus' throne as far as the eye could see. Waters in Scripture symbolize multitudes and multitudes of people. The sea he saw was not raging. No wind or waves. No storms. It was like glass because it was totally at peace. Every person who has been drawn into relationship with the One who sits on the throne can live now and eternally in complete peace. So think about that, and begin to commune with your Friend the Holy Spirit to bring the atmosphere of heaven into the waves, the storms, or winds you or your loved ones may be facing right now.

COME UP HIGHER

The Holy Spirit desires to create hunger in us that draws us into a state of living with Him in that atmosphere. He wants to break the cycle of struggling with things we cannot seem to conquer. Difficulties, rather than leading to defeat, present the opportunity for a demonstration of His glory. Small beginnings will have big finishes when your Friend, the Holy Spirit, is invited to invade. As He comes, we receive His wisdom, His counsel, His enabling, His power, His miracles.

There is nothing greater than seeing the miracle of a life transformed as God in you and through you shares His love, healing, salvation, encouragement and purpose by His Spirit.

It is our prayer that as you have read this book, you have come to love more and more deeply the Person of the Holy Spirit. He is the Friend who will always be there and never let you down. He is the One who knows who you are and the glorious future you were created for. He is the bond of Love that brings you to your heavenly Father and prepares you as Jesus' spotless and perfect Bride! He is the Comforter who heals and makes you whole. He knows all things, and you can rely on Him to lead you to magnificent destiny. He is the omnipresent, omnipowerful, omni-knowing Promise of the Father. He is God.

The testimonies you have enjoyed in this book are a tiny sample of greater things God has stored up for you. He is ready to meet you where you are and take you up higher.

Let's pray right now and welcome the Best Friend you can have in this world and the next to fill you anew with His presence and awaken your whole being to His voice, His love, His gifts and His power to refresh your body, heal your heart, strengthen your mind.

Prayer

Spirit of God, in the name of Jesus Christ, I honor and worship You. I want to know You more and more every day as my Helper, Counselor, Comforter, Teacher, Leader, Companion and Friend. Help me to yield my life to Your leading and tune my ears to hear, Father God, when You speak. Awaken my heart to Your wonderful presence. Heal me and transform me in Your glory. May Your love, Your gifts, Your power, Your authority flow through me so I will carry the atmosphere of heaven wherever I go for myself, for my family and for those around me.

About the Authors

Mahesh and Bonnie Chavda have been ministering with their Best Friend, the Holy Spirit, for over 35 years. In that time more than a million people have come to salvation and thousands more have received healing from physical, emotional and spiritual brokenness. Both Mahesh and Bonnie carry a desire to see believers around the globe fully awakened to their purpose for living, walking in power, abundance and joy in every area.

Bestselling authors, Mahesh and Bonnie have written more than a dozen books, including the Hidden Power series and *Make Room for Your Miracle*. The Chavdas are co-founders and senior pastors of All Nations Church in Charlotte, North Carolina, and Atlanta, Georgia. They also spearhead a global prayer network, The Watch of the Lord™.

Chavda Ministries International
P.O. Box 411008
Charlotte, NC 28241–1008
Phone: (704) 543–7272
Fax: (704) 541–5300
Email: info@chavdaministries.org
Website: http://www.chavdaministries.org

800-924-0047